For the Love
of a Mother

For the Love of a Mother

THE BLACK CHILDREN OF ULSTER

Annie Yellowe Palma

THE CLOISTER HOUSE PRESS

First published in the United Kingdom in 2017 by
The Cloister House Press

ISBN 978-1-909465-56-5

I dedicate this book to

My mother Ivy Yellowe (nee Gracey)

My father Frank Peter Yellowe

*My brothers – Jimmy Gracey, Alan Gracey,
Gabriel Yellowe, Wilson Yellowe and William Yellowe*

My daughter Paris Palma and my two grandchildren

Nia and Nieyma Palma

Special thanks to Gabriel and Wilson for their support
and encouragement.

About the Author

Annie Yellowe Palma is the only girl and middle child of six. Her father was Nigerian and her mother Irish. Her parents separated when she was about 4 years old and she never saw her father again. He died in 1968. Her mother died in August 2008.

She is a Qualified Social Worker with a Diploma in Social Work, a BSc Honours Degree in Applied Social Science and an Advanced Award in Social Work.

During the 60s and at the height of the troubles in Northern Ireland, we were the only black family living amongst what I refer to as, the 'Irish Mafia'. The 'Mafia' members include individuals belonging to both the Protestant and Catholic paramilitary factions.

This story is an account of life in Ulster through the eyes of a black child, exposed to the daily struggles associated with the civil war then.

In 1986 I made a life or death decision and moved to London to escape the madness.

I chose life!

Lest we forget

The Yellowe's are part of the history of Ireland, never to be forgotten and to be remembered always.

This is my journey ... come on, walk with me ...

Contents

The Lord's Prayer

Our father who art in heaven
Hallowed be thy name ...
As we forgive those who trespass against us
Lead us not into temptation
But deliver us with all evil ...

"From all evil," my best friend Didi giggled nudging me in the ribs and opening one eye to squint at me.

"Oh fuck, no wonder I've had such a shit life, I thought it was, WITH all evil," I replied in horror. Didi was killing herself laughing all the way through assembly, but I couldn't even concentrate and she thought I was joking.

I lay in bed that night contemplating the idea that I might have given myself some awful bad luck by reciting the Lord's Prayer wrongly. What if I really had brought on this shit life by getting it wrong? I vowed that from this night on I would do better, after all "could do better" was what all the teachers wrote in my end of term reports. From now on I will say the Lord's Prayer every night and emphasize, "Deliver us FROM all evil."

What if God thought I was taking the piss? I thought it couldn't hurt to try to put things right with God and try to change my life in the process. Get the Lord's Prayer right and my life will change, I thought as I stifled a yawn. Sleep pulled at my eyelids and I succumbed happily knowing that tomorrow things would be different for me, better. Living a shit life and all because I got the words wrong ...

Chapter One

Meet the Family

My mother, Ivy Gracey was born in Northern Ireland or 'Ulster' if you come from a staunch Protestant family, as she did. Because of the North, South divide and the war about who owned the land, Protestants made sure to always distinguish themselves from Catholics and vice versa. No-one ever said they were 'just Irish'. You were either from 'The Free State' and a nationalist, a Catholic or fenian, a taig or simply green, or from 'Ulster' and a loyalist, a Protestant, a Prod or simply orange.

Whatever the religious persuasion, each guarded their own territory with ferocity. Just in case there was any confusion as to whether you were entering a Catholic or Protestant area, the kerbs on the pavements were painted either green, white and gold for the former and red, white and blue for the latter. Further to these reminders, there were painted wall murals displaying local and historical figures revered as heroes in the eyes of the artist and their particular community. Amongst the apparent favourites were Billy Wright (former Unionist activist) and Bobby Sands (former Nationalist activist and hunger striker) to name a few.

I didn't understand the politics and have always had a very simple view of the world, live and let live. I certainly didn't want to kill anyone because they were different, not the same as me. Most people weren't the same as me and

1

although my friends and family patted me on the head trying to reassure me, "you're one of us," I didn't feel like one of them. I was aware of my difference and struggled to understand it. I wasn't interested in the history of Ireland, I had one hell of a job just being black and I wanted to know more about my own history.

1966 saw the formation of the Ulster Volunteer Force (UVF) a loyalist paramilitary group; and the start of 'the troubles' (the war between Catholics and Protestants) and the cycle of sectarian killings began. As a young child, I was vaguely aware that prior to 1966 Catholics and Protestants had lived alongside one another. However, because of simmering fears about the government of Ireland violence eventually erupted between the Irish Republican Army (IRA) and the UVF. There was talk of the ruling Queen becoming a 'turn coat'. This was an expression used when a Protestant became a follower of the Catholic faith and vice versa. Apparently, the British Government were not taking seriously the complaints of Irish people about who should have a say in how Ireland was governed. The point being that the Nationalists (Catholics) wanted the British Government to have less say leading to a Free State and the Unionists (Protestants) being against this as they feared this would lead to the break-up of the United Kingdom. I didn't understand what all the fuss and fighting was about but I used to join in the song we kids sang about 'The Queen'.

In nineteen sixty-six
The Queen pulled down her knicks
She licked her bum and said yum yum
In nineteen sixty-six

Ivy lived with her mother, two brothers Billy and Wilson and her sister Winnie. They shared a tiny two up, two down house in Florence Court, Portadown, County Armagh which is approximately twenty-three miles south-west of Belfast, the Capital. Mum had told me that they saw little of their father, Billy Gracey, who fought in the second world war and had the medals to prove it. My grandfather had a strange accent, half pirate and half Northern English. He said things like, "Are thee stoppin the night" meaning, are you staying here tonight. Even as an adult, no-one else appeared to notice this but me. When I discussed my observations with my brothers, they thought he might have picked up bits of other accents due to being in the army and moving around.

If you didn't know my grandfather, he appeared distant and cold. But we knew he was quite a character, funny and caring. He wasn't good at showing his softer feelings and would comfort us by holding us with outstretched arms and kind of woodenly saying, there, there, from a distance. If we were rude or naughty, he would demand my mother beat us. As soon as she lifted her hand he would jump between us and tell my mother, "not that hard". I don't remember him ever lifting a hand to me or any of my siblings. I loved him so much and when I wanted to hug him, even though he tried, I wouldn't let him get away. He would laugh as I huddled him into submission for an awkward hug. I'd try to kiss him on the cheek, and he would gently turn his head away and kiss my forehead, patting me on the hand from a distance. Grandad looked kind of bemused by me. Although I never heard him say he loved me, I think he did. My granddad showed me affection to a point then he just couldn't go further. I'm quite sure he never bargained on having to deal with black people or little black children. So, whenever I lunged at him to shower him with affection, it must have been quite a shock. Our histories so different, our stereotypes hung by a thread, yet we were connected by blood, by duty by life.

My grandmother Annie Gracey, who I was named after, had died in her early fifties. My mother, then a teenager, had already gone to live the high life in Ipswich with a girlfriend. There was an old black and white picture of grandma that took pride of place on my grandfather's living room wall. My mother was her living image. Much to granddad's fury, we used to join my uncles in teasing him about finding another woman. My grandfather never spoke about her except to indicate occasionally that no-one would ever replace her, and no-one ever did. Many times, my grandfather would sit next to the big open fire smoking his pipe. I loved the sweet pungent smell of that tobacco and enjoyed watching the clouds of smoke swirling up to the ceiling. It reminded me of my own father who was by this time a mere shadow in my mind, all his identifying features, gone. I would be sat next to him whilst he stared at my grandmother's picture in complete silence, with a lop-sided grin. The silence only momentarily broken by the loud and gentle 'tic, tock, tic, tock' of the big grandfather clock and the occasional shrill chirp of his caged budgie, Joey.

I asked my mum how my grandmother had died and rather than answer me she stared into space and said "she had nice hands." She was clearly reminiscing but I was far too young to understand. I became confused and thought this was the reason she popped her clogs. I thought it was quite strange to know that having nice hands could kill you. They should warn people about the dangers of having nice hands, the way they put warnings on bottles of nail polish, or on packs of fags. I bit my nails to the quick thereafter...I didn't want to suffer the same fate! Mum told us she didn't have the money to travel home for the funeral and she was devastated. To lose her mother was bad enough but being absent from the funeral and having missed the opportunity to say 'goodbye' or 'I love you' was terrible.

My grandmother's death had a profound effect on my mum which manifested in many ways. Not for the first time and without warning she was off upstairs again to her bedroom. I crept up to the door and stood outside listening as she cried silently into her pillow calling for her mum. "I want my mother, I want my mother," she cried pitifully as she rocked back and forth. I couldn't bear it any longer and opened the door. "It's alright ma, I'm here, I'll help you darling," I soothed. I reached out and held her, saying everything would be fine. I felt helpless because I couldn't get her mummy for her. My mum's body shook as she sobbed, her long dark hair stuck to her tear stained cheeks. I wiped her tears away with the sleeve of my cardigan. It was a long time before mum stopped crying but eventually she pulled herself together and returned to being my mum. "Alright darlin, mummy's ok now, let's go back downstairs love." I don't think any of my mother's family knew how she was affected by her bereavement, it was as though she cried in secret. I observed that when my mother wiped away her tears, she often did this as though she was angrily, defiantly, ripping them from her face. As though she was

5

trying to show some invisible person or people that she wasn't broken.....that she was strong and would survive her mother's passing in her own way. Maybe that's one of the reason's she turned to alcohol.

When mum was drunk, she used to sing a song she said reminded her of her mother.

When you lose the one you love
How lonely life can be
With such a memory . . .

My mother drank a lot, smoked up to forty cigarettes a day and could be heard regularly and happily effing and blinding about good or bad situations. For instance, if you were wearing nice clothes, mum would comment, you look fucking gorgeous. If you pissed her off she would tell you to go fuck yourself. Oh no, she didn't mince her words. She was quite small and slim and very beautiful with a wicked sense of humour. She could fight too and tore the hair from the heads of many neighbours. You had better not get on the wrong side of her because if you did, you would not forget her acquaintance in a hurry.

When my mum wasn't binging on alcohol she was fine. She was attentive and loving and always ready with a comforting word or two.

"Look ma I've hurt my finger on the chair," I wailed in agony.

"Oh, poor wee darlin," she comforted.

"Bad chair, bad chair," she shouted whilst thumping its sides. "Don't hurt my wee ba again," she scolded whilst holding me tight and kissing my finger gently. I felt great knowing that the chair had gotten a good beating from my ma. I felt secure knowing that the chair would not hurt me again and I felt proud that my ma loved me and could protect me from chairs and monsters and ghosts. We certainly needed protection because the adults around us told us so many harrowing ghost stories and made us believe in horrible myths until we were shaking with fear. I carried illogical fears with me into adulthood about death, ghosts and all manner of made up fuckeries.

My mother told me that she was quite wild and restless when she was younger. She was always looking for excitement. She told us she was a bit of a tearaway and not easy to control. I often wondered how her life was before her father joined the army. She was thirteen years old when her father went to war and nineteen when he returned. I think not having their father around much as teenagers had a negative effect on all my mother's siblings. They all drank and smoked quite heavily and my two uncles never left the family home until they were very much older than would normally be expected. The youngest, uncle Wilson, left in his forties to live with a Catholic woman despite the family's staunch Protestant background. I don't think granddad bargained on this. My older brothers Jimmy and Alan had lived most of their young lives with my grandfather. Alan left shortly after uncle Wilson, when he married and had his first child, Daniel. The oldest, uncle Billy, never actually left the family home. I don't think my grandfather bargained on having an elderly unmarried son around him. In his late sixties and never married, my uncle Billy finally moved out of the family home when my grandfather died in his eighties.

My mother had already run off to England with a girlfriend making her way to Liverpool where she met and married my father Frank Peter 'Iyalla' insisting this was how he first introduced himself. This was much to the annoyance of her family who had been through the trauma of having to deal with the earlier embarrassment of her having two illegitimate children. They had further been forced into a position where they had to confront and manage their feelings about a little human not of their kind, a black child. My mother told us harrowing stories about how her father and brothers threw her out in the street when she had Alan. I was very shocked and angry when she shared the stories with us. We cried together as she shared how she had to sleep on the sofas of various friends. I felt sorry for my Alan being carried around from pillar to post, not wanted by his family. I felt sorry for my mother being ostracised in such a vicious and uncaring way by my grandfather and uncles. Were these the same people who professed to love me?

My mother clocked my expression and began watering down the impact by telling me, in the end they warmed to Alan and her. Those stories made me more insecure and conscious of racism and I planned to watch my family's reactions to us and listen for any clues to their racist views. After my mother's revelations, I had a profound distrust of adults although this was to save me from harm and possible abuse on many occasions.

Having already had Jimmy out of wedlock, when she had Alan, her family must have gone mad. Having a black child whether married or not must have been a great disappointment to the family full stop! Poor granddad, probably suffering from undiagnosed post-traumatic stress disorder linked to being in the army and fighting on the beaches of Dunkirk, then having to deal with illegitimates, darkies and fenians! I sat listening with tears in my eyes in disbelief and hoping for a happy ending. I was always hoping for happy endings. Mum said one night out of the blue her family invited her round. They studied Alan for a while before lifting him up and understanding that he was just a little human being, an innocent child who needed and deserved to be acknowledged and loved! The rest as they say is history and Alan was never far from my grandfather's side thereafter.

During one of her many stories about 'daddy' mum said he had run away from his family in Port Harcourt, Nigeria in West Africa. My mum pronounced it, Portacourt. After years of family research undertaken by my brother Gabriel, he confirmed the true pronunciation. We heard how dad had stowed away on a ship to England when he was nine years old.

"When the captain caught him, he was beaten to within an inch of his life," she said sadly. I felt sorry for my poor daddy and I wanted to kill that captain for hurting him. "Another man who was travelling on the ship found out what the captain had done to your dad. He was very angry and he went and found the captain and kicked the shit out of him. This man then ensured your dad made the rest of his journey to England in safety."

"Why did the bad man beat my da," I asked tearfully.

"Well in those days, white people didn't like black people love," she replied, as a matter of fact. According to mum, Frank was twenty-three years older than her, a merchant seaman, an amateur boxer 'Frank Honeyman' and a chronic gambler who smoked 'funny fags' or 'white cigars'. It dawned on us years later that these 'funny fags' were actually joints of cannabis. During his research, Gabriel also found out that my father was actually, a professional boxer representing Birmingham from 1921 to 1925. We've never really known much about my father, except that he was our father. Well he fathered four of us, well maybe, three of us. Funny though only two of us look alike. Anyway, the Irish always told us, "Sure you darkies all look the same."

"Aye, your father was born Tamina Wila Buka and his father was the first policeman in Nigeria, or was he the king of a tribe?" She never could quite remember the story, maybe it was the drink. "Oh, bottle take effect," she sang in a drunken haze. The drink was "the very thing to numb the pain," she said. The drink was "the very thing to block it all out and forget for a while," she said. I was always puzzled when mum said these things because I didn't know what she meant by pain and needing to block things out. We were the ones who knew what pain was. Mum was in a constant drunken stupor as we suffered from her neglect. We needed something to help block it out ... Oh, for the love of a mother!

She and my father parted and reunited regularly. My mother shuffling us back and forth from Liverpool, where I was born, to Ulster. We awoke one cold dark morning to the vision of mum rushing around in a panic. Shoving clothes into bags she told us in a hushed voice, "Hurry and let mummy get you ready, we're all going on a lovely trip to Ireland." Wilson was carefully but firmly stuffed into a blue padded romper suit. The suit was too small for him and his arms remained upright as mum placed him still asleep into his pram. The suit ended just above his little ankles and he looked stiff. Gabriel and I looked on sleepily and yawned, oblivious to what would follow.

Once out of bed we huddled together for warmth. Our clothes as usual too thin for the weather and the rain was relentless in Liverpool. It was hard not to be listless and miserable and we were always cold. In desperation, I used to put my cold bare feet up the back of mum's jumper to keep them warm. We were frequent visitors to many other houses. Mainly we were dragged by our mother from house to house where she indulged in heavy drinking sessions with her cronies. The commonalities between these people being alcohol and miserable looking children who were cold and often hungry. I don't ever remember seeing such a thing as central heating. We saw many big open fireplaces but none had fires lit. The grates were dark and empty where there should have been orange embers emitting terrific heat.

We were out the door in a flash with no thoughts about my father. I hated Liverpool with its tall grey buildings, never ending rain, and air of depression. This big grey stone cobbled monster was about to fade into a bad memory and although we didn't know it then, replaced with evermore harrowing memories of our young lives. Every street mum dragged us down smelt of either fish and chips signifying an English community or coffee and goats milk signifying an African community. I was excited and confused. I was nervous as well as I could sense mum's anxiety. We didn't know at the time but she was trying to get away with us before my father came home from work. By the time he'd return to our home, we'd be long gone. Without a word, not having said goodbye or I love you and we would never see our father alive again. Ring any bells?

We had sensed mum's desperation to get away the day before. My parents were arguing again and the shouting woke us up. Through sleepy eyes I had seen my father pushing my mother against the big wooden dining table in the kitchen. Big kitchen dining tables manufactured to aid social gatherings, communication and eating one's dinner. I don't remember eating at that table or sitting around it like normal families were supposed to. There was a pot of strawberry jam on there and not much else. The jam toppled onto the floor and the jar broke open. There was a lovely sweet smell and I was sad that we wouldn't have bread and jam for breakfast. Tension remained between my parents and later that day my father had sat me on his lap whilst on his favourite chair near the fire.

My father was about to light up his pipe. "Can I hold the match daddy," I asked. My father nodded and smiled down at me. "Frank, don't let her do that, she'll burn her wee hands," shouted mum. My father didn't seem to hear her and he continued to guide my hand and the match towards his pipe. My tiny hands trembled but I managed to ignite his pipe. As I retrieved my shaking hand the red of the match burned into my finger and I cried out in agony. "See, what did I tell you," mum roared with rage as she dragged me from my father's lap. My father didn't bat an eyelid. He showed no sympathy but continued to suck on his pipe quietly watching mum and slowly blowing the smoke up into the air.

"I need some money to get home," we heard her say to a dark brown gentleman whose flat she had taken us to. During mum's conversation, we ascertained that Alec was a friend of my father's. He had big yellow teeth and a wide smile and his eyes seemed too big for their sockets. Alec looked well fed and his belly hung over his belt. He seemed unruffled by mum's desperate plea for help. He was rather jovial with a slight air of superiority about him. "Now let me guess, this must be Annie get your gun," he laughed extending his fat brown hand to ruffle my hair. I was just about to violently shove his hand away when I noticed the glint of money between his fingers. A false smile immediately replaced my facial gurn.

"Here you are my dear, go and buy some sweeties."

"Oh, no Alec, I wouldn't let her go to the shops on her own," said mum protectively.

"That's alright Ivy, there are some kids playing downstairs and they will take her."

Mum looked annoyed. She didn't want to be bothered with having to see to me and my sweets, she had business to do. She reluctantly took me downstairs to where a group of kids were playing in the hallway. "Love, would you take her to the shop across the street for me please." The kids screwed up their faces and one looked to the other to answer. They clearly didn't want to take this stranger to the shops. Eventually and under mum's intense stare, one of them said she would take me and mum leapt back upstairs to Alec leaving me at her mercy.

As soon as mum had disappeared the young girl's smile vanished. "I'll show you where it is, but I'm not taking you all the way," she snapped. "Oh, that's ok I can find my way back by myself," I offered just a little too convincingly. I wanted them sweets bad! "Come on then, hurry up." She rushed me across the busy road and walked a little way with me before giving me instructions to turn left at the end and then right, cross over the road and the shop is at the end of the street. Easy, I thought. "Thanks," I shouted as she skipped off again. I was so pleased with myself for being able to follow her instructions and soon found myself outside the sweet shop.

The dark brown wooden door was already open and I stepped inside. I had to stand on the tips of my toes to peer over the counter. The shopkeeper didn't appear pleased to see me. "Yes, how can I help," he barked. He was small and fat with pale white clammy skin and his belly was much bigger than Alec's. He made me feel so nervous and rushed and I ended up choosing the nearest thing to me so as not to make him angrier. "A bag of Maltesers please," I stammered. He grabbed a packet with his stumpy hands and threw them on to the counter. I had trouble stretching up to reach them. He sneered at me with delight as I struggled, deliberately not offering his help. Perhaps he was playing a game with me but I eventually managed to grab them between the tips of my fingers. I trotted out of the shop with my booty thinking, "Fat bastard".

Once outside I instantly became aware of an older boy sitting on a step across the road. He was looking directly at me and smirking. I became afraid and thought he was going to approach me, maybe take my sweets or something. Did she say left then right or right then left? I questioned myself. I didn't quite yet understand my left from my right. I'd nodded my head to all her directions just to get to the shop, the rest was just blah blah blah. I was in a state of panic and confusion as I struggled to remember what direction I had travelled to get to the shop in the first place. I began having tickles in my chest, like little butterflies, but they hurt me. The pain grew as the boy stood up on the step like a lion homing in on its prey.

I thought I should look confident in case he tried following me." I skipped to the right of the shop trying to appear as if I knew exactly where I was going. Out of the corner of my eye I saw the boy sit down again like he'd lost interest. I felt relieved and smug that I'd tricked him into thinking I knew where I was going. I began tucking into my sweets. I passed a big wall and I remembered this. I walked along feeling confident and relieved. When I reached the end of the road however, the familiar block of flats that I expected to see had somehow disappeared. I didn't see and couldn't hear the voices of those same children from Alec's block.

I felt a gush of hot blood rushing to my face and my chest. I quickened my step searching for something familiar, something that would jump out and tell me I was safe again. I wanted my mum's arms around me right now! I wanted to smell her smell, I wanted to see her face. "Where are you mummy?" I whispered to myself. I became more and more lost and confused. Floods of hot tears stung my cheeks and my nose started running. I was so afraid that if any of the 'bad men' mummy often told us about saw me crying they would know I was lost and come and get me.

As I blindly stumbled down yet another unfamiliar street, like a scene out of a horror story an old white lady approached me. "She might be a witch," I thought, "but I need help, I need my mummy." "Are you lost my dear?" she asked in a shaky soft voice that made me believe, "yes she is a witch but I just have to trust her."

"I want my mummy," I cried as I sucked my bottom lip in and out furiously.

"Don't worry dear we'll find your mummy for you," she said as she stretched out a long skinny wrinkled hand to comfort me. I could see her long finger nails were dirty and wondered what was in them. I flinched from her touch. "Now which direction did you come from," she asked. That was not a good question to ask and if she didn't know where I'd come from, well, I was doomed.

The witch can't help me and I'll never see my mummy again. I was shaking uncontrollably in floods of tears. It was getting darker, I was all alone on the street, my mum nowhere to be seen and me with a witch who was going to do some evil to me any moment now. I couldn't speak, I was in shock. I just kept shaking my head, "no, no, noooo". Right now, I hated sweets, I wish I'd never been craven for them in the first place. I almost threw the rest of the Maltesers on the ground, but even in such a distressed state, I couldn't let that packet go. As the witch shifted her bony body in my direction I resigned to my fate.

When I opened my watery eyes the witch was still there but a miracle was happening. "It can't be," my heart skipped a beat. "It is, it is ... muuuuuuuuuum." I was hysterical and running now. My mummy was coming towards me. She was pushing the big bouncy pram hard and walking fast. I couldn't see who she had in the pram but the big white blankets were bouncing up and down furiously with her every step. A policeman was beside her trying to keep up. I started running and now she was running too. My mum looked pale and frantic as she reached out to me . . . safe at last.

I looked behind me and in an instant the witch was gone and I was being snuggled in my mum's warm arms. I felt her tears on my cheeks as she kissed me over and over. "I thought I'd lost you, I'll never trust those horrible wee bastards again, excuse the language son" mum raged through her tears. "Thank you, officer," mum wailed as she stretched out to shake his hand. "You alright now sweetheart?" the policeman asked with a smile. "Thank you for bringing my mummy to me," I replied. A little girl at the tender age of four walking the streets of Liverpool alone, it could all have ended very differently . . .

Ireland beckoned and mum was not about to let anything get in the way of that last boat. Each street mum dragged us through had its own unique character and smell. When I could smell fish and chips I'd get excited and thinking we were already in Ireland I'd ask, "Are we there yet mum?" "Not long now sweetheart," she'd pant. I was too young and innocent to note that we had only walked a short way from our own home in Liverpool. We tried to dodge the gunge stuck to the cobbles. Most of it was old newspaper that had been used to wrap up the fish and chips from the night before. The papers were strewn everywhere and now lay sodden with traces of stale fish still evident.

The streets were very similar to some of those I remembered in Ireland but when I asked, mum just kept saying that we weren't there yet. My little legs were tired and I was out of breath but mum pulled us on regardless. She was on a mission and staring straight ahead in the direction of the sea. I was so looking forward to seeing Jimmy and my granddad again and having fish and chips with them. It was such a long way to Ireland. I smelt coffee and goats milk and knew instinctively that we were still in Liverpool. Some of the houses mum made us stay in had these distinctive aromas. We were not used to goat's milk and even when we were starving with hunger, mum would have a job trying to get us to drink it when she had no cow's milk to give us.

Down yet another street and the smell of dried fish threatened to choke us. We held our mouths as we passed any areas where it was sold. I hated that smell and thought that if I trotted faster we would get to Ireland quicker. I wanted to be away from the goat's milk that came in strange long bottles. I wanted to be away from the grey. I wanted to be away from Liverpool and those strange people we had to share our lives with including the fish eating, fish smelling Patterson's who loved goats milk.

Just before mum and dad's last fight, she had taken us to stay with the Patterson's. They lived in a small basement flat in a sprawling period building with their five children. I remember being fascinated that we had to go downstairs to get into their home. The twins from next door were watching. Two dark skinned girls with eyes like bubbles in a piss pot and their pigtails tied up in white ribbons. They looked immaculate. Their skin was creamed to a perfect shine and I could tell they were well fed. It's amazing the things you notice at four when you're always hungry. It was hard to tell one from the other as they wore the same matching outfits.

Blue checked dresses that stopped just above their knees, long whiter than white socks that looked silky and smooth and beautiful white sandals, the kind we could only dream of. They watched as we navigated our way down the steep steps. As I looked up from the bottom step, one stuck out her tongue at me. "Charming," I thought, "dressed to kill and no manners." I had no concept of basements as I was used to walking into my home at street level. "Do they live in the garden mum?" I asked in a state of confusion. "Don't be silly and watch your step," she replied.

At tea time the children's father Apo tried to force us to drink the dreaded goat's milk. I put my hand over my mouth and wouldn't touch it of course. Mum came to our rescue. "Oh, they don't like that milk Apo do you have any cow's milk love?" Apo was not very pleased with us and said, "You're too soft Ivy, if they were mine they'd bloody drink what they were given." He then commanded that his older son Mannie take us to see if old Darlington had some cow's milk. We passed the bemused faces of the twins again and this time I stuck out my tongue. I wanted to put dirt on their socks with my foot, just a little bit, but my brother hauled me away by my sleeve before my foot made contact.

Having descended a set of steep steps to another dark basement, Mannie, Gabriel and I huddled together at the bottom. Mannie knocked loudly on the door. Sometime after, we heard a shuffle. Eventually the door was opened by an old man who could hardly breathe. He had huge lips that dripped when he spoke and he was very dirty. His jumper did not quite fit over his huge belly and his feet hung out of holes in the sides of his shoes. "Look at Darlington's big black toes," whispered Mannie.

We put our hands over our mouths to stifle the laughs. We were quite frightened by the sight of Darlington and couldn't believe that Mannie would dare make fun of him so blatantly. Darlington shuffled back to us with a bottle of cow's milk and we leapt back up the steps. "Mannie, weren't you frightened he might hear you?" I asked. "Darlington is ok. He looks like a monster but he's very kind and sweet," he replied. I shrugged, at least we wouldn't have to drink goat's milk but I would have nightmares about the sight of that poor old man.

After tea, we watched the children plaiting each other's hair. Babs, the oldest girl tried to show me how to plait but I was hopeless. As she held her youngest brother Jofi on her lap he wriggled and I noticed some scar tissue on his back. "Oh, my God, what happened to him Babs?" Babs told us that she had been playing a swinging game with little Jofi when he was much younger and she had accidentally let go of him. She'd been twirling him round and round as he giggled with delight and to her horror, she flung him straight into an open fire. I felt sad, what bad luck, a fire that was lit for a change, yeah bloody bad luck. He was such a lovely, lively little thing and it was hard to believe what he'd been through. I so wanted to cuddle him but he was too shy and would not venture too far from his sister.

When we stayed with the Patterson's they made us go to bed really early so Apo and his wife Fola could indulge in boozing with my mum. Apo was the head of his house and his word was law. "Come on you lot upstairs," he commanded. His children filed out quietly and obediently with their heads bowed and their eyes averted from his in fear of his temper. We didn't even get to kiss our mum goodnight. Apo quickly disappeared back downstairs locking our bedroom door behind him. We were distraught and frightened because the room had no light. Gabriel and I clung to each other in terror as we banged on the bedroom door screaming for our mum. Mum never came and when we collapsed onto the floor exhausted from crying, that's where we woke up next to each other the following morning.

My bones hurt and I was cold and hungry. When mum finally showed up she told us, "I couldn't let you come downstairs last night because when Apo switched the light on there were cockroaches everywhere, hundreds of them crawlin all over the floor." We shivered in disgust as she went on, "do you know that he makes his poor wee children sleep in their school uniforms so no time is wasted in gettin them off to school in the mornins?" "Are their clothes all wrinkled we asked." Mum didn't need to answer. The children filed out of the house in their creased shirts that were once white and black trousers that had gathered at the bottoms through wear and tear. They looked hungry, sad and depressed and with their plaits sporting bits of white fluff from the bedding. There was no noise, no cuddles goodbye and no breakfast offered, I felt sorry for them. In fact, I began to think about those scars on baby Jofi's back and other possible and more sinister causes. I had thought it odd that he constantly clung to Babs who supposedly caused his horrific injuries.

Mum walked so fast we had to trot to keep up with her as she expertly weaved the huge bouncy pram and three small children through Liverpool's grey cobbled streets towards the Docks. Once on board the ship mum went to get us some drinks with threats of, "now sit still and don't move a muscle or mummy won't bring you somethin nice." The excitement of being on a big ship was too much for us kids and as soon as her thin frame was out of sight, we made our way to the side. The night was cold and everything looked darker and greyer than ever and it had started raining heavily.

The ship swayed from side to side amidst the huge expanse of water that violently sprayed us now and then and threatened to drag us overboard. With wide eyes, we continued looking on in amazement at the big grey watery ghost. Lots of people were looking at us and murmuring, "Where's their mother?" "They shouldn't be out here alone, it's dangerous." Some of them began to crane their necks attempting to spot our mum. They shook their heads as if disgusted at the lack of parental supervision.

Gabriel caught a glimpse of mum returning and we shot back to our seats. I was very unsteady on my feet. "My belly hurts," I moaned. Everything went fuzzy and I felt I was being spun around by an invisible person. "Here Annie this is for you," she began, as I heaved the contents of my stomach into her lap and all over the floor. Oops, sea sickness. People were shaking their heads again but mum was completely oblivious and went about the business of cleaning me up. I spent the rest of the journey with an empty belly and I was the colour of a corpse. We were freezing on the ship and when we talked, smoke came out of our mouths. I snuggled up close to mum and under the wings of her coat that she had opened to comfort me. The journey passed in a haze of sleepiness.

Chapter Two
Coming to Ireland

The train finally chugged to a halt in the old station at the corner of Watson Street. Ah the bliss of Florence Court, the smell of the chimney smoke, the back to back houses and the promise of poverty. "Hello son, look at the size of you," said mum cheerily to Jimmy who came to greet us. He was lanky and white and my mum's first born. Jimmy had long brown hair that always seemed to cover his bright hazel eyes. I remember his beautiful smile and his love of the Beetles. Mum later told us his father was an Irishman but Jimmy knew nothing about him. He called our grandfather 'da' which was the short Irish version of daddy. Jimmy was strong and helped us with our bags into a house with the number 31 on the front door.

A sea of white faces jostled to see the spectacle of Ivy and her wee darkies moving in beside them. My second eldest brother Alan lived with Jimmy, my two uncles and my grandfather in another two up, two down several doors away in number 17. Mum later told us that Alan's father was a black American soldier who he knew nothing about. He too called our grandfather 'da.' Alan had soft black curly hair, light brown skin, the cheekiest twinkle in his dark brown eyes and a passion for football. "Did you bring me anything ma?" enquired Alan. Mum waved him away with a look of disappointment. "Here we are escaping from Liverpool and you're asking for presents," she tutted.

"This is not bad," said mum as she walked around inspecting the tiniest living areas I've ever seen. We had two small bedrooms at the top of thirteen steep wooden steps. The journey upstairs was dark and my legs ached from climbing. The stone yard was very small and contained a big brass coloured water tap that hung loosely off the wall and to the right of that a toilet. Both the yard and toilet were cold and uninviting. When I saw the state of the toilet seat I was not looking forward to putting my arse on that! Directly to the right of the toilet was a concrete coal shed or 'coal hole' as mum called it, with a tin roof. This was dark and empty apart from a few pieces of coal lying amongst the dust that lingered in every corner. When we opened the door, we sneezed as the dust worked its way up our nostrils.

Directly at the bottom of the steps that led to the bedrooms was the kitchen. It was tiny with a cold concrete floor, no windows, and a huge white square sink with a crusty old water tap attached precariously to one wall. Mum called the kitchen 'the scullery'. One step away from the kitchen was the living room. The floors were red and cobbled and it was so cold I think we were warmer outside. There was a small window that had a thick white cleaning solution smeared over it, to keep out the nosey neighbours, mum had sniffed smugly. "Boys, take off the children's coats while I light the fire," mum commanded. I held my coat tight. There was no way I was letting it come off or I would truly freeze to death. "Ma, she won't let me," Alan protested. Mum told him to leave me and come and help with the fire. We watched as she twisted up bits of old newspaper placing them in the grate. The boys had brought a little parcel of wooden sticks and she put some of these on top.

Mum disappeared out to the yard for a few minutes and returned with the pieces of coal we'd seen hiding in the corners of the coal hole. She placed the coal on top of the wood and set light to the newspaper. We heard the crackling sound of the wood catching light. Mum asked Alan to hand her the 'poker'. Alan handed her a long steel rod that she pushed under the paper. She told us that was to let the air into the fire to make it blaze. "Close the doors and keep the heat in," she shouted. We soon began to feel a little warmer but we walked in a peculiar manner on our heels to avoid fully putting our feet on the cold stone floor.

Jimmy was to go and get some bread, butter and milk from the corner shop so we could have tea. We were quite used to eating bread and butter and not making a fuss. Alan piped up "is that all they're gettin ma?" Mum said we'd be fine and he was to stop asking questions because he was doing her head in. She lit up one of her long white Parkdrive cigarettes, and inhaled deeply. There were no tips on these cigarettes and mum would smoke until the last bit of the 'butt' burned her fingers. Her thumbs and fingers were yellow with nicotine stains.

We ate our bread and warm tea as our brothers looked on. "Look at the state of your face," mum shouted, "get over here." Then with the end of her dirty apron plastered in fresh spit, she lovingly drew this all around my face, I wretched at the smell. God help me, she nearly got my mouth. I don't know what was worse, the smell of the nicotine on her fingers or the smell of the spit.

"Remember Gabriel," mum asked. Alan knew all of us because he had lived with us in Liverpool for a while before my grandfather had come to bring him to safety and some kind of normality. Alan later told me my dad was a 'c**t' and he hated him. Alan was like my mother and didn't mince his words. He too could fight and you dare not unnecessarily cross him. Alan wrinkled up his nose and eyed up his brother. Gabriel had dark brown skin and eyes that shone as bright as his lovely white teeth. We were all blessed with pearly white teeth. I have no idea how that happened because the last thing on my mum's mind was brushing our teeth or any kind of dental hygiene. None of us owned a tooth brush either. The Irish told us that all darkies had white teeth. So, I guess it was just a darkie thing then. It seemed to me that there were some benefits to being a darkie.

A few years later Gabriel, or Giggy, as we often called him, was to become quiet and watchful after a terrible road accident that left one of his friend's dead. One bright sunny, Sunday afternoon, Gabriel went with his friend Rod and his little sister to buy ice lollies. On the way home from the corner shop, they had to cross the main road that was always busy. As they stepped into the road, there was an impact that threw them all into the air. Gabriel was knocked unconscious, but the little girl was dragged under the car and tragically, she didn't survive.

Gabriel loved toy guns and pine cones and didn't eat sweets. Now that was weird. What child in their right mind would not eat sweets? Didn't I lay my very life on the line for Maltesers back in Liverpool? After me, Wilson was introduced. Wilson had honey coloured skin, the same soft black curly hair as Alan and the same mischievous smile. He later showed affection for money and trouble and wore several scars on his head because of his recklessness. Wilson was a survivor and if he needed something from you there was no escaping him. If your back could be described as a ladder to success, he would be climbing the rungs six at a time, to get up to the top of your neck just before breaking it. Everybody loved Wilson, he had a charm the rest of us lacked. We spent the next few months getting to know our neighbours and soon settled in. Despite our obvious differences, we had something in common with the street kids, we were all poor and almost all the parents drank alcohol in excessive amounts whether openly or behind closed doors.

On a dull September morning, we woke up and noticed mummy had a big belly.

"Why is your belly so big ma," I enquired with the innocence of a baby goat about to be slaughtered.

"Oh, I ate too much food," laughed mum.

"Right you lot, upstairs ordered Adel, one of mum's neighbours.

We were ushered upstairs and told not to utter a word or come out of the room until we were told. We huddled together the way we used to when we stayed at the Patterson's. We were confused because mum and her cronies had not been drinking. After a while I could hear my mum panting loudly and grunting. We put our ears to the door and heard the distinct sound of a cat meowing. The cat must have been very hungry because the meowing got longer and louder. "What the hell is going on down there," I wondered. I didn't bloody like cats and I didn't want one living in my house. They looked evil to me with their slanting eyes that shone in the dark and their clingy, scratchy claws that held your clothes when you wanted to throw them off.

27

When we were finally allowed back downstairs, there was no cat to be seen but there was a little brown baby in mum's arms, a woman in a white dress and a big brown suitcase perched on the window sill.

"Where did that baby come from ma?" I asked in amazement.

"The nurse brought him to us in the suitcase," she laughed.

"Is it ours ma, can we keep it?"

"That's enough now, don't you be askin your ma any questions," warned Adel, dismissing us with the look of Atila the Hun.

William Samuel Yellowe mum named him. We called him Billy or wee Bill and he was a result of one of mum's return trips to Liverpool. He was the youngest and the cutest. He had Wilson's honey coloured skin, the soft black curly baby hair, mischievous eyes and a beautiful smile and giggle. He loved snuggling, baby food and ma's diddies. The fun we had when she squirted us with the diddy milk. Ma had a good aim and boy she could squirt quite a distance and with great accuracy. We often collapsed on the floor in fits of laughter with, "I surrender, I surrender, no more ma, no more." We used our sleeves to wipe the diddy milk from our eyes and watched as the squirter bit disappeared into Billy's hungry mouth.

The woman in the white dress came to our house a few times after Billy was born. "Now Ivy, you know you can't be drinkin alcohol when you're breast feedin." "What? Oh, good God no Evelyn, no. Sure I wouldn't do that. I hardly touch the stuff now anyway," mum lied. "Make sure you top and tail him regularly," Evelyn shouted as the front door closed behind her. "Top and tail? Tail? Oh, perhaps Billy is a cat after all. No, he can't be because he doesn't have the slanting eyes and I can't see no tail either," I assured my brothers. I thought I would keep an eye on him though in case he turned into a cat. Lovely and all as he was I didn't want his wee nails clinging onto my clothes thanks.

As soon as Evelyn's arse was out of the door, mum laughed as she retrieved the carefully hidden bottle of Mundie's wine from behind a well-placed blanket. By bedtime, my mother was drunk. We had to rescue Billy from her as she held him upside down on the bed trying to put a nappy on his head. I'd heard his little meows and ran to mum's room. "Ma what are you doing?" I shouted. She mumbled that she was "changing the chile's nappy." It's a good job I'd watched her when she was sober. At that moment in time, everything else paled into insignificance, my drunken mother, the poverty, the fact that I myself was a young child.

My mother was slumped on the bed and with her eyes closed. My eyes were wide open and I became totally focussed on the task at hand. The only thing that was important to me was making my little helpless brother as comfortable as I could. The instinct to protect him was so strong. I laid the nappy out on the bed in a triangle and placed Billy's wee arse in the middle or there about. I pulled the three corners together around his little bum. He was so wriggly and I was frightened that I might stab his delicate skin with the safety pin I held. My hands shook but I finally managed to fix the nappy in place with the huge safety pin. The nappy was a bit wobbly but I felt it would be alright until the morning. I stood there for a few minutes not knowing what to do next. Then I carefully put him back in the bed right next to my mother's drunken frame and tucked a blanket around him. Many times in the night I heard thuds, then Billy meowing. I rushed to mum's room to rescue him time and again. He just kept rolling out of bed as she was too drunk to support him in her arms. I couldn't sleep for worrying and I prayed to God that he would survive the night.

Billy was growing fast and he soon became accustomed to the neglect we knew so well. He was a tough little cookie and as soon as he was picked up off the floor he would start cooing and smiling as if all was normal. "How are you surviving you wee trooper," I sang into his little face. In a drunken stupor mum would whisper, "Billy's father is not yours. Oh, and his father was Joe Miles, the first black policeman in Liverpool." I think she had fantasies about powerful men or men in uniforms. I couldn't imagine a policeman holding my mum in a romantic clinch with the vacant look she wore after a drinking binge and the smell of piss on her person. "How could any man in his right mind find that attractive?" I mused. It hurt me when my mother told me this. The first time she said it I was confused being too young to understand relationships. When I grew older, my mother confirmed Joe Miles was Billy's father. We laughed it off but I think it began to affect the way Billy related to us as he got older. When we were fighting, and being spiteful with one another, we liked to remind him he was, 'not one of us.' We didn't mean it though and just did it to crush his feelings in the moment.

"Ma, you dropped the chile last night," I said accusingly whilst pointing my finger in her face.

"You're kidding me," she replied laughing.

"No ma. You could have killed him."

"What was I doin love."

"Tryin to put a nappy on his head." She laughed until she coughed.

"Look at him he's as strong as an ox."

"It doesn't matter ma, you could have killed him."

"You're right daughter. I'm gonna stop drinkin."

"You always say that ma."

"I know love, I know. But this time I mean it."

Her words were so convincing. I really wanted my mum to stop drinking and I wanted to believe her every time she said she would. I had good butterflies in my stomach all day in school. Perhaps my mum would even come and meet me outside the school gate, like other mothers did. Sometimes my mum walked us to the local bus stop and we travelled the rest of the way alone. She never ever came to pick us up. I felt sad about that. Sometimes I felt angry and embarrassed as other children and their mothers stared at us trooping in and out of the school gates alone. Sometimes my mother was so hung over and didn't have the energy to walk us to the bus stop. On these occasions, we had to stay at home. The days long and dark, reflecting my mother's mood.

Not today though. Today my mummy would be sober and the world would be brighter. Today I might even get a proper cooked supper. I had no money again for the bus and I skipped the two miles home from school with hope in my heart. As soon as I entered my home, the bad butterflies ate my stomach from the inside out. Billy was crawling around on the cold dirty floor with his nappy dirty and full, the weight making it hang off his bottom. The stench was terrible. I thought about how this little innocent child must have been literally on his own all day long. What must his life be like when I'm not around? The worry of this constantly played on my mind in school. No wonder I couldn't concentrate, I couldn't think straight, the bad butterflies constantly gnawing my stomach even when I put my hand there to try and stop the pain. I couldn't think childlike thoughts because I was too busy thinking about my mother drinking and neglecting my baby brother and I was overwhelmed with anxiety wanting the day to finish so I could rush home to him. I realised, I was the mother of three, yes, me, still in primary school and already performing a mother's role. I knew I wasn't a good mother but I was a mother, I had no choice. When things were not right my brothers looked to me, waiting for me to make everything better. How could I let them down? They would have been lost without my immature mothering skills.

Billy looked up at me with his big bright eyes and reached out for me to pick him up. Mum was lying on the sofa unconscious and with an empty bottle beside her. I felt physically sick and the bad butterflies just wouldn't go away. Through the hot stinging tears, I cleaned the baby up as best as I could using an old sheet because there were no clean nappies. I'd learned these tricks from my mother. When she'd drank all the money for essentials such as food and nappies, she used to tear up old sheets, pillow cases and anything she could make a nappy out of. The main thing keeping Billy alive was probably mum's alcohol laced diddie milk. I carried him to a neighbour and begged for some milk as mum was clearly not in a state to put the diddie in his mouth. I wish I'd thought of mastering how to attach him to the diddie while she slept.

The neighbours were quite used to us begging for things and aware of the possibility that my mum might be in the house drunk. "Where's your ma?" asked Maggie. "Drunk," I replied. "Here love, take these." Maggie shook her head sympathetically as she handed me some milk, some bread, some biscuits and some coins for chips. I was frightened to go to my grandda because he'd threatened my mum with the welfare officer or the 'cruelty man' earlier that week. Granddad often told my mum that if she continued to neglect us he would have us taken away. Mum had cried and promised, "May God strike me dead," that she would stop drinking and take care of us properly. I began to wonder whether most people were like my mother. Our street seemed to be full of people who drank heavily, pissed themselves in and out of their own homes and who were very violent.

A common utterance at the drop of a hat was, "I'll fuckin kill you." Like the times when we couldn't sleep. We lay top to toe in two beds. The mattresses stank of urine. When drunk, mum pissed, any place, anytime, anywhere, just like in the Martini advertisement. We shared three thin blankets that were once white and were now dark cream with some interesting stains. When mum gave us a good beating, I tugged at those piss stained blankets until they covered my whole body. They could still do a good job of preventing the sting of a lashing belt as mum rained down blows on your arse and legs for messing about or making noise. "When I put you to bed, you go to sleep, or I'll fuckin kill you" she would spit in a rage. "But ma, it's only six o'clock and all the other children are still playing on the street." She just missed my face with the buckle as I pulled the blankets up in time to ward off the next lash. The blankets weren't washed often, which was just as well, as the dirt added to the weight and made us feel warmer. On very cold nights when mum was sober and thinking straight, she would put newspapers and coats on the beds to keep us warm or at least this would ensure that rigor mortis didn't set in overnight. I don't think anyone would want to murder their children by freezing them to death.

Sometimes I was thankful for the after effects of a good beating. Crying is exhausting and sleep inducing. It was hard to get to sleep without a dose of the 'lilac liquid' or a beating, because we had mice. I'm not boasting because everybody had mice, they weren't ours exclusively. They were little buggers, uninvited guests, and part of daily life. I used to comment on how fat they were, but mum said in our house their bellies were likely to be extended through malnutrition...mal nu what? I didn't know what that meant. Surely big bellies mean full bellies? "They have big bellies because there's nothing to eat at the Yella's residence," mum scoffed. "Big bellies like the poor wee starvin African children you see on the telly," she added. I remember lying in bed shaking with fear as I listened to them scratching at the floor boards. I thought they would crawl up the bed and eat me. They were quite the little performers and many a night we watched as they scaled the curtains.

"I'm gonna kill those dirty little bastards." Gabriel hated the mice with a passion. When left to look after us, he and his friend Gordy would set traps for the mice. They were quite creative. They used an old hairnet laced with cheese.

Obviously, the cheese came from Gordy's house. There could never be cheese that didn't get eaten in our house and if we dared to put it in a mouse trap my mum would have used the buckle of the belt to make sure you didn't do it again. Gordy lived next door with his grandfather who was the best story teller on our street. He was handsome and we used to play kiss chase with him. Not one word could be uttered by anyone when the trap was set. Hours would pass as we watched the mice 'nearly' get caught in the net. The only sound was the faint flickering of flames peeking out of the bright orange fire. The heat of the fire and the quiet ambience enabled us to lure the mice into a false sense of security. I think the mice came into our house because they liked the smell of the wine my mother and her cronies drank.

The famous words were uttered again the time I got blood all over the floor. Mum shouted, "what have you been up to (like I was capable of committing mass murder). Get in here and wash your hands, or I'll fuckin kill you." I tried to explain where the blood had come from. I'd heard Tracey shouting, "Annie, my dad's skinin eels, you wana come and watch?" "Eew, skinin eels where?" I had asked skipping inside the front door. Tracey led me into her yard (where all murders seemed to take place) and there stood her father Ray over a huge metal bucket of wriggling eels. Ray was tall and fat with red cheeks and a deeper voice than Barry White. We watched as he cut off the heads. The long glinting knife crunched through the neck gristle. Ray used the same knife to expertly skin the eels' bodies before placing them back in the water that had now turned red with their blood.

"Look Ray, they're still moving," I screamed. Ray laughed and told me they were dead. "How can they be dead when they're still moving?" I felt sick but Ray just continued cutting and whistling. "Your dad's a cruel bastard," I whispered to Tracey. "Da, she say's you're cruel." Ray put out his big hand that was the size of a shovel and grabbed me with his fingers that looked like big fat pork sausages. He forced my hand into the bloody mix and I screamed. "Go on Annie, feel them wriggling. Look, they've no heads." He laughed until his big red ruddy cheeks looked like they would explode, then collapsed in a coughing fit. I managed to pull my hand free of the sausages and I ran outside with my bloody hand held in the air like it didn't belong to me. "Ah sure he's just jokin with you," said my mother when I told her between sobs about, "that mad man."

"Look ma, I caught my good anorak on the door." I'd torn my navy-blue anorak trying to get away from old sausage fingers. "Don't worry love I'll fix it," my mother assured me. "Go on down to your grandda's and ask him if he has any blue thread." My grandda didn't have blue thread and he sent me up to ask Iris the seamstress. Iris was a large fat lady with a squint in her left eye, a heavy Scottish accent and a very pronounced speech impediment. She was loved by everyone in the street and was expert in mending clothes. Bad luck though because Iris didn't have any blue thread either. "Oh ma, what am I gonna do, I've school tomorrow," I wailed. My mum asked me to take off my coat and get her the only thread we possessed which was white. "You can't sew a blue coat with white thread," I protested. "Watch this," said mum.

When she had finished sewing the tear she put her hand up the inside of the chimney pot and withdrew it with soot on her fingers. I looked on in a state of confusion wondering why she'd put soot on her hands. Mum began to spread it over the white thread being very careful not to smear it on the coat. "See, your auld ma's not daft. What about that love?" It wasn't great, but I had to admit it was better than the shame of wearing a blue coat with white stitches. I didn't like Ray for killing those poor wee eels and wiping their blood on me.

So, it appeared everyone was capable of murder. I knew that people beat their children; I'd heard the screams and seen the evidence in the form of bruised eyes, cuts, fat lips, flinching and the look of fear in some children's eyes when their parents raised an arm to scratch their nose. I never actually heard of anyone murdering their children though. Orla, one of my Catholic neighbours called me over when I was playing out. I was doodling on the pavement with a piece of chalk, fantasising as usual about a normal life and generally minding my own business. "Annie, come and see this." I liked Orla. I immediately threw down the chalk and ran over to her. Orla led me quite roughly by my hand into her yard. Her husband Shaun was there and seemed busy chopping something. "Oh, my God they're lovely," I cooed as he stood back from a bundle on the ground. Their Mindy had just given birth to six cute little puppies. They were all huddled together, protecting each other and keeping warm. It reminded me of the many times me and my little brothers huddled together for the same reasons.

I asked why there was blood on the sheet that covered them. Shaun shifted uneasily as he explained how he had to cut their tails a bit shorter. I cringed to think of the pain they might have been in but Shaun reassured me that they "don't feel a thing because they're too young." Again, this reminded me of the times people tried to make us think that black children don't have feelings like white children and their parents don't care about them the same way white parents care about their children. I thought whether you are a wee puppy or a black or white child, we all have feelings and we can all feel pain. I felt sick because I just knew those wee puppies had felt the pain of that knife searing through their wee tails and Mindy looked sad. "We are keeping them Shaun, right?" asked Orla. "We'll keep them for six weeks, wean them off Mindy and sell them off," replied Shaun. "Can I have one Shaun?" He looked scornfully at me and replied, "Sure where would your ma get the money for a dog, she can hardly look after you lot." Orla and I laughed because although that hurt, it was true. As I was leaving, I heard Orla and Shaun arguing over the price of the pups.

I vowed to speak with my mum. I would buy one of those poor wee pups because Shaun didn't understand their pain and I felt sorry for them. The next day I hovered gingerly around my mum to gauge what her mood was. If she had a massive hangover and I asked her too soon she would be certain to shout, "I'll fuckin kill you." Mum was in a jovial mood and I thought it might be a good time to ask her about having a pup. "Is he givin them away?" she asked abruptly. "No ma, he's sellin them," I replied. "What? Sellin mongrel mutts, sure who in their right minds would buy them?" I couldn't believe my luck, Mum asked me to go over and bring one so she could have a look.

The door was open and I took the liberty of letting myself in. Shaun and Orla were out in the yard standing over the bucket. "Oh Annie, now's not a good time love," Shaun shouted as he tried to stop me from entering the yard. "But my ma wants to see the pups Shaun." Orla looked up and I could see her eyes were red from crying. "What's the matter Orla?" She didn't answer but ran out of the yard calling Shaun a, "fuckin murderin bastard." Shaun pulled the sheet off the top of the bucket and to my horror the wee pups were inside. The bad butterflies consumed me and I felt faint. "Shaun they'll drown," I screamed. Shaun was well aware of their fate. He moved around as if all was normal, "They were no good love, not pure breeds" he said shaking his head. The little bodies floated around in the bucket of water that was stained with blood. I was absolutely devastated. I wailed into my hands at the thought that I couldn't save them. Running out of the yard I stepped on an old newspaper. There was something rubbery under there. A breeze caught the newspaper exposing the wee pup's mutilated tails. "You are a fuckin murderin bastard Shaun." I didn't know it then, but this would be the last time I ever set eyes on either Shaun or Orla again.

"Get up, get up, it's been snowing," I yelled to my brothers. We peered through the window amazed at the white blanket. It wasn't long before all the children in the street came out to play in the snow. We built a snowman outside our front door. Having placed the last bit of snow on his head I ran crying to my mother because my hands were frozen.

"Ma can you buy me some gloves?"

"God help you love, you think I've money for gloves."

"Just a cheap pair ma."

"Here put these on." She handed me a pair of socks.

"Oh ma, they're lovely and warm."

"Look, my ma let me have socks for gloves," I giggled to my friends.

Before we knew it, our friends were sporting the same sock gloves. We had a great time throwing snowballs at each other. We made a go-cart or as we called it, a 'gig' out of an old pram using the wheels, a long plank of wood and some string for steering it. It was very difficult to stop in the snow but we held on to the walls to help us to slow down when necessary. Things got scary and reckless as the older children joined us. They put stones inside their snowballs and raced down icy hills whilst hanging on to moving cars. One by one we were called back inside by our mother's. I couldn't move my fingers. "Oh Jesus Christ, feel her wee hands," mum cried into thin air. "Let me put water on them," she added. To my relief, mum poured some nice warm water onto my hands and in an instant, they began to thaw out. I got up on the sofa behind mum and put my feet up the inside of her jumper. "Oh Jesus, your feet are freezing," she laughed. My toes were cosy in no time.

"Because you've all bin so good, we're gonna have a treat tonight," said mum smiling at us. We whooped with delight because treats meant biscuits. When we'd changed into our bed wear, knickers and vest, mum produced what we'd anticipated, a great big packet of Vienna biscuits. They were triangle shaped wafers, covered in chocolate and with a vanilla cream in the middle. "No way, she's got three and I've only got two," wailed Wilson. "There's not enough to split them evenly now stop fightin," scolded mum. "No way," shouted Wilson before grabbing one of my biscuits. It wasn't long before all hell broke loose as we fought the good fight over biscuits.

Mum calmly took all our biscuits away from us and without another word she crumpled them up and threw them into the blazing red fire, pushing them into the embers with the steel poker. Why oh why did the fire have to be lit tonight? We cried so hard we couldn't breathe. In between sobs we accused each other of being greedy and blamed each other for the loss of those beautiful biscuits. It was gut wrenching to watch them burn and the smell of the melting chocolate drove us mad. "Don't fight over biscuits in this house like fuckin savages," mum spat before herding us roughly upstairs to bed. Our bellies were hungry again but we only had our savage selves to blame.

I was feeling anxious because mum was going out later tonight. Mum was hyped to the gills and nothing could dampen her spirits today. A familiar shadow appeared in the window. In she stepped with her big bouncing titties, mad red hair, her limp and her never ending stories about boyfriends who turned out to be married men. Melandra Allen was the streets unofficial hairdresser. Melandra thought she had the look of Cilla Black about her. I thought she looked like more like Bernadette Devlin. Give her a glass of port and a listening ear and you could be rewarded with a free and meticulous hairdo. Melandra had a whining voice and when she was on a roll, even the mice could be seen committing suicide by freefall off the curtains. Her laugh was shrill and her whole body shook as she joined my mum in celebration at getting rid of that 'bastard' before his wife found out. She had bony fingers and nails deformed from being bitten to the quick. It was interesting to watch her expertly twisting the rollers around any unsuspecting wisps that strayed from mum's head. When she'd finished with the stories and the curling, Melandra always had a satisfied but manic look about her.

Mum's scalp looked taut and unnatural but she had good decorum as the pain always made her walk perfectly upright and with a stiffened back. She complained of having a headache until the rollers were removed. Her complaints fell on deaf ears as Melandra cackled loudly. I tried to warn mum that she should stop encouraging Melandra to talk about the 'bastard men' when she was having her hair done. I was convinced that this was Melandra's twisted way of getting revenge on these men. The rollers symbolising their plump little bollocks and the pin that held them securely, her imaginary knife! I told mum that every time she winced in pain I could see that Melandra's eyes went funny and she laughed uncontrollably. Mad Melandra was probably thinking, "Yeah, feel some of the pain that I feel you bastard man." "Here Melandra, take this," mum said. She put her hands down her bra and took her purse from it. "No, no Ivy, that's alright," said Melandra waving mum's money away. Mum put the purse back safely in her bra next to her cigarettes.

I'd watch her getting ready to go out drinking. She would boil some water in a pot and pour it into a plastic bowl. Like many others, we still didn't have a proper bath or a bathroom. The kitchen door would be half closed for privacy and I'd peep through the crack to see my mum washing her bits. You are probably familiar with the three

'R's… reading, righting (writing) and rithmatic (arithmetic). Well, when washing herself, my mum practiced the three 'F's… face, fanny and feet. Mum told us lots of stories about the Yanks in the war time and how she acquired nylons. The Yanks were suckers for my mum's good looks and those batted eyelids. The nylons were later replaced by Candle Glow tights and when mum sent you to the shops to purchase a pair, you'd better not get it wrong, only Candle Glow would do.

She seemed in such a hurry to get out. Her thick black hair was stripped of pipe cleaners. Mum used these to curl her hair when Melandra was away with one of her bastard men. The pipe cleaners were long pieces of white cotton wrapped around a thin wire. They were cheap and very effective. After removing the pipe cleaners, she combed her hair into a wavy mass. On went the dark tan face powder that immediately filled the house with an unforgettable perfumed smell. This was followed by black eye pencil on her eyebrows and the inside of her eyelids. Mum didn't actually have any eyebrows as she'd shaved them off years ago, in a drunken stupor, but there was a kind of grey shadow where they used to be and this acted as a guide to her swooping pencil. She then put a dot of ruby red lipstick on both cheeks and furiously rubbed it in to create instant blusher. That same lipstick would be applied heavily to her thin pale lips, just a little above and below her lip line for a fuller effect. The final touch was a black mole on her chin. Mum always insisted on painting this mole on her face. She said it made her look classy and film star like.

"Oh fuck me, nearly forgot me tits," laughed mum. She

produced a set of rolled up socks and pushed them inside her bra adjusting them until they were just right. Six children and years of breast feeding had taken its toll and mum had flat pancake diddies. She stood in front of me, adjusting and readjusting her skirt. "This too short, too long?" she'd ask into thin air. "Far too short mum," I'd yell in disgust and attempt to pull it down. My stomach churned, it's not that I didn't want her to go out, I just didn't want her to come home drunk. Because I knew that when my mother was drunk that almost certainly meant we would be witnessing violence between her and Elvid Astan. She'd met him at the local pub and began letting him come around to our home. He would go on to wreck our childhood and caused us the most terrifying suffering behind closed doors.

"Wait until you see what I've got for you," she promised. Mum returned from the scullery with a large bottle I was familiar with. She proceeded to pour a pale lilac liquid into my open mouth. "There, you like that don't you," grinned mum. It tasted bitter sweet and I crinkled up my nose as I swallowed. This was prescription medicine that was supposed to be used for calming colic in babies. Anyone in the street who had trouble getting their kids to sleep used it to force them into an almost instant coma. The label read, one teaspoon to be given. I don't think my mother could read because she gave us two tablespoons. After the second spoonful, I heard someone in the distance saying, 'Give her some more.' My mother's face was getting bigger and I couldn't see her properly, but I heard her say, 'I don't want to kill her.' I'd beg her, "please mummy, don't go, please don't go." My speech becoming slower and mumbled as the liquid cunningly soothed my brain making me feel warm and fuzzy. She never listened to my slurred pleas though. She just pulled her skirt up a bit shorter and darkened her red lips.

My brother had to hold on to me as she tried to get out of the house. I rugby tackled her thin legs trying to stop her from getting away. "I'll be home in half an hour," she shouted as her made up face and black glossy mane disappeared out the door. She always said this, but she never did come home in half an hour. I'd lay awake fighting the sleep-inducing effects of the medicine, waiting to hear the familiar steps coming down the street. Dozens of people walked down our street after the pub closed but I could pick out my mum's footsteps with ease. I'd lie very still, listening and eventually my heart would miss a beat and skip out of control as I heard the familiar stilettos. Click, click, clickety-click. Oh God, here she comes, my mummy's home. "Mum, mum," I shouted with joy. On the rare occasion when she wasn't drunk, I'd curl up beside her in bed and whisper, "I love you mummy, I love you," then I'd silently cry myself to sleep, overwhelmed by her sobriety.

Chapter Three
Family Life

Wash day and mum had no money as usual, so it was the big tin bath boiled on the cooker today. There was something quite comforting about watching my mother doing ordinary things like washing. On these occasions family life felt bearable, real and I felt loved. I was proud of my mum and in awe of her strength and determination to get chores done and to a high standard. She looked like she enjoyed the challenge too and this was proof she could do normal motherly things if she chose to. She would stagger out into the yard and balance the huge bath of hot water on a chair. In minutes the air was filled with the smell of green fairy soap. The whole street smelt of green fairy soap which was used for everything, washing your hair, your body and when it was necessary, for de-constipating you!

"Get me the soap," mum would squeal if we dared mention constipation. We would then be made to squat over the toilet whilst she softened the soap in warm water and rubbed it on your arse. To much relief, the old bowels would immediately open up and let loose the last ten days of gunge. My mother would look on triumphantly as if she had waved a magic wand or plunger. There wasn't much time to contemplate dignity, the remedial soap was just accepted as was the fact that your brothers watched on huddled together and in stitches at the sight of your arse up in the air with bubbles floating out of it.

The scrubbing board was removed from under the heavy white sink in the kitchen. With its wooden frame and glass ridges all the way down, it lifted off any stains as well as a good deal of mum's skin, and she always had blisters on wash days. The washing line was soon crammed with nappies, socks, knickers and shirts, having been forced through a rusty old mangle. Mum would stand back with sweat dripping from her face as she smoked another cigarette. Half way through the cigarette mum had to go to the toilet. She rested the long white bit of the cigarette on the cooker with the red glowing hot tip sticking out over the end of the knobs. As soon as she was out of sight Gibb and I were at the fag.

I took it up carefully making sure I didn't burn myself and put the white bit in my mouth. It was wet from mum's lips. I sucked a little and coughed as the smoke pounded my lungs. My mouth tasted horrible and I quickly passed the fag to Gibb. "Hurry up before she comes," I warned. Gibb repeated my actions but having smoked more times than me, he didn't cough. I was jealous and promised myself I would try harder next time. Mum appeared and looked at us suspiciously. "Did anyone touch my fag?" she asked. "No way ma we wouldn't touch your dirty fags," we lied.

Right, now she was in the mood for some proper work. The tin bath was up on the cooker again. We were lined up in the living room and one by one we were well and truly scrubbed. I jostled to be first because I hated the thick black scum that accumulated around the sides of the bath signifying lack of previous. When mum was in this mood, we dared not upset her for she was intent on finishing the job. So, if we whimpered that she was tugging our hair too hard, she would hit us on the back of the head with a spoon. "Sit still or I'll give you something to cry for," she'd scream. "Ma that towel is soakin wet," I yelled. "Go in the wash bag and get me a shirt," she commanded. Off I went to the big black bin liner in the scullery.

As I opened the bag I had to hold my breath when the stench of dirty clothes tried to crawl up my nose. I reluctantly felt around the bag until I found a shirt that was not too dirty and only smelt a bit. I quickly returned to my mother and handed her the shirt. Mum rubbed me down and I was dry in seconds. There was a slight smell of arm pit odour on my body where the shirt had left its mark. The shirt was dragged over the bodies of my little brothers leaving them with the same whiff. We were then taken into her bedroom to have our hair examined and fine combed. I shuddered with revulsion to see the fat brown lice reading the news of the world as they were evicted from our heads and onto the huge sheets of paper.

When the pain in the back of my neck became unbearable from leaning over the newspaper, I would try to get away. "They will carry you to the River Bann and drown you like a rat," mum threatened. I was horrified at the thought of being drowned by the lice, and a little impressed they were strong enough to lift people up. I put a vice like grip on my neck attempting to dull the pain as I endured the rest of the head exploration. "Ma, can we have fish and chips tonight?" I asked. "Where would I get the money for fish and chips," she replied, taking out the frying pan. "You never let us have anything nice ma," I said sulkily. "I bet we're adopted cos I don't think you love us." My mum laughed until she nearly choked. "Adopted? Adopted? If you were adopted, I'd have no hesitation in bringin you back to your own ma tomorrow. I wish you were adopted." This hurt, but deep down, I knew my mother didn't mean it. Hadn't she brought us from Liverpool when she could have left us with our father? Hadn't she kept us even though she could have allowed the cruelty man to take us? Hadn't she saved us, when she was approached at a sea-side resort, by a couple who asked if they could have two of us? They had followed us around all day and when my mother noticed and asked why, they said how lovely we were and how they longed to "have one or two." Then they offered my mother money for Gabriel and me. She looked a little bit scared and refused pulling us close to her.

"You love Elvid Astan more than you love us don't you." She had mentioned Elvid to us a lot and we were sure he was going to become her 'fancy man'. My mother wasn't even listening now and continued busying herself in the scullery. After a fried greasy egg and a sausage, it was off to the urine soaked beds upstairs. She was quite the singer was our mum. We laughed till our sides ached as she tried to sing us to sleep. We wondered where she got the lyrics from ...

Three little darkies lyin in bed
Two were sick and the other half dead
Sent for the doctor the doctor said
Mammas little babies need shortnen bread
Shortnen shortnen shortnen bread
Mammas little babies need shortnen bread

In bed, all lullabied out, we could hear mum frantically scrubbing the front doorstep. When we peeked out of the bedroom window, we could see that the step was bright red. Every house had a half moon of red concrete placed outside the front door directly on the pavement. It was a source of pride and joy to have this sparkle. When thoroughly scrubbed, wax was applied and mum would straighten her back and walk into the house as if we owned a mansion. Manically cleaning was one of my mother's ways of coping when she couldn't get her hands on any booze. The lack of alcohol and thinking about it would drive her crazy and cleaning took her mind off it for a short time.

"Can Annie come swimming with us Ivy?" asked Mabel, one of my older neighbours.

"Annie, you wanna go swimming with Mabel?" mum shouted.

"Yes ma, will you gimme the money to go?"

"Mabel, I haven't got no money love, but bring her across to her grandda, he'll give her some."

"Don't worry Ivy I have the money for her."

I loved going swimming with Mabel. She was so lovely and really looked after me. I changed into my blue swimsuit, the one with the blue flowers on and squeezed my afro under my blue matching rubber cap. Granddad had bought these for me and I loved them. After putting our clothes into a locker, we headed for the pool. "Careful love, don't slip," Mabel said as she took me gently by the hand. We had to pass through a shower to get into the pool. This shower was to ensure you were clean enough to swim. Many children used the local swimming pool to get a bath and I'm sure some of those filthy little bodies did not see water other than on swimming days, mine included.

The shower was a rude awakening and absolutely freezing. I tried to skirt around the sides but the spray caught me on my back and shoulders. I screamed out and shivered uncontrollably as the water ran down my head and back. I stifled a, "Fuckin hell." Mabel was not accustomed to hearing wee children swearing and thought I was an angel so I didn't want to disappoint her. I jumped into the kiddies' pool which was lovely and warm, like a bath. The water came up to my chest when I stood up. Mabel stayed with me for a while teaching me how to swim and playing games.

"Right love, I'm off to have a swim in the big pool." I didn't like it when Mabel left me because the bigger girls from my street would taunt me if they saw me alone. "You'll be alright sweetheart and I'll be back soon." I was having a great time 'doggy paddling' across the pool when suddenly there was a huge splash followed by loud laughter. Four of them were in the water before I had time to pull myself out and run for Mabel. "Alright Annie?" asked Jade, who lived on my street. She was usually not a threat to me, but she could be an unpredictable, scary and spiteful bully when she chose. Later in my secondary school I had watched her many times beating other girls to a pulp in the toilets. Jumping on them without warning and savagely punching anywhere they couldn't shield before dragging them by the hair onto the ground to bang their head on the stone floor and against the sinks. Other girls standing around in a circle egging her on. There was spit, hair and blood everywhere. I listened to her boasting of her blow by blow accounts afterwards. I used to look at her and think about how her life must have been behind those closed doors to make her such a violent person. She looked so pretty but masculine and with long brown hair. Jade liked to listen to the blow by blow accounts of other boys who had regular fights in school too and it appeared she liked to copy their brutality. "Let me see how you can swim like a big girl now." I didn't want to show her because I knew this was a ploy to get me to let go of the long silver safety bars around the pool's sides. She looked annoyed at my reluctance and sidled up to me ripping my hands away from the bars.

I was pulled under by my legs in a flash. I panicked and came up spluttering and coughing and fighting for air. I momentarily heard the laughter again before disappearing below for the second time. On resurfacing my body was shaking as I held on to the silver bar trying to get some air into my lungs. "Please don't, please don't," I spluttered. Her hands were like two huge lumps of concrete on my shoulders as down I went again swallowing a huge gulp of water on the way. When I came up again I vomited. My head was spinning and my chest felt as if someone had hit me with an iron bar. I was so weak and I thought I was going to die.

Although none of the other girls tried to help me or stop my absolute distress, one eventually relented, "alright, alright, leave her now, do you want us to get thrown out?" I was relieved and having sucked in some air the tears streamed down my cheeks. "Oh stop with the tears, we're not gonna touch you, you cry baby." Just then a security guard came over. "You alright love?" he asked. I didn't dare answer because the big girls were staring at me, daring me to tell him and warning with their eyes what would happen if I did. "Yes, I'm alright, I just slipped," I lied. The guard could see my distress and could guess what had happened.

"Right you lot out."

"But we haven't done nuthin."

"Out I said."

"Don't worry love they won't be botherin you no more," he soothed.

"Where's your mum?"

"I'm with my friend. She's in the big pool."

"Show me who she is love. You shouldn't be in here without an adult, ok?"

I heard my name being called just before the girls exited through the shower. When I looked up Jade who'd tried to drown me drew her hand across her throat with an invisible knife. The earlier sickness in my stomach turned to bile and hate. I so wished I could batter that bitch to a pulp along with her henchwomen. The guard brought Mabel to my rescue and when the girls caught a glimpse of her they ran like the wind bumping into each other in their attempts to get out fast. Mabel asked why I hadn't called for her. "They kept pushing me under and I couldn't get my breath," I cried. "Oh love, I'm really sorry. If I see them outside, I'll kick their bloody arses." I'm glad I didn't die that day because Mabel bought me a lovely bar of toffee and a packet of crisps on the way home.

In March 1969, the British army arrived to save us from our enemies, and each other. Rioting was the norm and the streets were increasingly proving too difficult to control for our local police. Bernadette Devlin, a known IRA sympathiser had become Britain's youngest ever female

MP, much to the dismay of the Protestant community. Barricades sprung up all over the place to keep the fenians out of our streets. Hijacking was the new normal behaviour and house to house searches became part of daily life. Saturday morning was bright and the birds were singing. We were wiping the sleep from our eyes and just getting out of bed to start the day. There was a commotion outside and a lot of rattling. We jostled each other to get a look out of the window. "They've hijacked something," gushed mum. "Be a good girl and go see what it is Annie," she urged. Off I trotted towards the lorry that everyone had surrounded. "Stand back there, give her a chance son, everybody will get some, stand back." The UDA had hijacked a lorry load of alcohol and were doing their duty, distributing it to the community. I hated alcohol but I just could not resist getting something for nothing. I helped myself to lots of bottles. "Don't want to get the same as everyone else, so I'll take the pretty bottles," I thought. I skipped back home overjoyed with my goodies. "Oh for God's sake love, they're mixers," shouted mum disappointed at my choice. I shrugged my shoulders, I hadn't a clue what mixers were, it was all booze to me. "She should be grateful," I thought, "these will keep her going for weeks." She read out the labels, "tonic water, pure orange, lemonade and lemon."

"These are no good to me love."

"Look ma they're in cute little bottles and the big boys got all the bigger bottles."

"Go and see if there's anything left love."

"No."

"Go to the corner and get Alan," mum shouted. She wasn't giving up and maybe Alan would be more choosey in bringing her the alcohol I'd missed. Although my mother loved alcohol, strangely, she had some pride and it was this that was stopping her from going outside to get the drink herself. She didn't want to be seen grappling with others competing for a free bottle of spirits. I skipped along to the corner shop where my brother and his friends hung out. He indicated he was busy and that I should go home. I think the words he used were, 'Oi, you, fuck off home, now.' Thoughtful and charming I know. De-coded and loosely translated he meant, 'go home love, there's gonna be trouble.' Hanging out at this shop had a sinister purpose. For it was here that the Protestant men hoped to catch sight of the Catholic men coming home from work. Protestants and Catholics did not go into each other's areas for fear of violence or even death.

However, there were a group of Catholic men who had to pass the Protestant barricades in order to get home. Every night they had to run for their lives. Some were not so lucky, and it was a sickening and terrible sight to see the results when one got caught. A huge crowd would gather around and kick, punch and whip "the fenian bastard" until either the police came to save his life or he managed to get to the Catholic side before collapsing. This same punishment was handed out regularly. I was so frightened and traumatised by the constant visions of violence around me. I wanted to run away and hide ... I wanted to live in peace surrounded by love. Although the madness was everywhere, I knew this was not normal and that other people lived differently. I wanted to find those people, but as a child, my desire to find and achieve 'normality' was limited to fantasising. I never believed that one day I'd actually escape from all this.

Jimmy was getting married and I was confused. Did this mean that he would have to leave our house? Who would look after us? Certainly not my mother. The bad butterflies tore at my guts more than ever. I put my hand on my tummy to try and quiet the butterflies but they stayed with me every day making sure I suffered the unknown. He was a good big brother and used to keep some order in our home. Jimmy wore the customary pointed toed winkle pickers and was always listening to the Beetles music. Jimmy bore a strong resemblance to Billy Connolly and was just as funny. He drove a white Beetle car, which we loved to ride in. Jimmy was like a father to us. He took us to exciting places, the seaside, on picnics, and he always bought us sweets. I'd lie on the sofa and pretend to be asleep when he came home at night. I liked to feel his big strong arms picking me up like a rag doll as he carried me effortlessly upstairs to my bed. I felt secure around him and I was not looking forward to him leaving us for Jessie, his wife to be. I didn't like that Jessie was going to take my brother, my saviour and protector away from me and my little brothers.

Before I knew it, I was measured up for my flower girl's dress. I felt important, yes, I had places to go and people to see. Jimmy came for me, not my brothers, just me and it was a wonderful feeling being singled out for something nice. The dress was made of dark blue velvet and ended just above my toes. This was co-ordinated with a white fluffy halo. We fought to place this halo on my little afro and finally the curls relented as it was balanced on my head. A long white fluffy hand muff, white socks and dark blue sandals completed the look. Everyone fussed over me and I felt like a blue fairy princess.

I begged mum to give me some money to let me buy a wedding present for Jimmy. "Don't worry," she said, irritated at my cheek, "he knows we have no money for presents." That was mum's answer to everything, no money. This was a special occasion, her son was to be married, surely, she could afford some little thing, I cried. Mum took me shopping that day and allowed me to purchase two tiny brass effect candlestick holders. Although I was only seven years old, I was embarrassed by this meagre gift and I was not looking forward to giving them to my brother. That night I stayed at his fiancée's house.

Her sisters fought over me. "She wants to sleep in my bed, no mine, no mine." It was a nice feeling being fought over and fussed about. I couldn't sleep before handing over my present. Everyone watched in silence as I handed Jimmy the present wrapped in best quality newspaper, the one that had acted as a makeshift grave for the lice being dragged out of my head the night before. "Ahhh," they said in unison before breaking into fits of muffled laughter behind their hands. I didn't blame them, it was such a shit gift and I knew that. I felt humiliated and I was close to tears when Jimmy assured me it was one of his best gifts and it would take pride of place on his mantle. It was just like my Jimmy, always able to comfort me and make me feel better, but I couldn't stop the tears.

The past few days floated around in my mind as I slept that night. I cringed as I remembered the look on the dressmaker's face when she glimpsed my dirty vest whilst fitting my dress. I flinched when I had to remove my shoes exposing a big hole in my dirty socks as I tried on some sandals. I cried with embarrassment when Jimmy's fiancée came to get me out of the bath and found that the water had turned black and scum had gripped the sides. There was no hiding the dirt either because they had a proper white bath, not a tin one like us. The final humiliation was the present and those laughing faces. The faces that didn't know what it was like to be me, poor, constantly embarrassed by my circumstances and unable to stop it all. Oh, for the love of a real mother, I lamented.

I woke up to a flurry of excitement. I was clean, and my body felt lighter. I had on new white socks, knickers and a vest and I was having bacon and eggs for breakfast. They whipped my afro up into a fluffy black mass then fought with it as they tried desperately to fit my fluffy white halo. A few desperate moves and two hair grips finally secured it. I felt like a million dollars as I floated down the path in my blue velvet dress, my fluffy white halo, my fluffy white hand muff and my shiny nine carat gold bracelet that Jimmy had bought me as a reward for being his best flower girl. The neighbours jostled each other to get a look at the 'wee darkie.'

I could hear whispers of, "Surely that's not really his sister, maybe she's adopted. Ahhh, look at her she's lovely. Give us a curl love," they purred as they tried to touch my hair. I had an air of superiority about me that day. I had the face of an angel and the mind of a devil. Don't touch the blue fairy princess I thought, after all, you lot are the peasants today. Away with ye! The things wee darkies can get away with thinking in their wee black heads and ignorant adults can't do anything about it. About the only place I could be private was in my own head. In my head, I could be anyone I wanted to be. I was usually posh with long hair and an English accent.

I couldn't believe my eyes when I saw my mum for the first time that day. She looked normal. Her hair was tied up and she was wearing a wide brimmed black velvet hat, a checked black and white coat and black gloves. Yeah, I would even say she looked rather sophisticated.

"Oh you look lovely ma."

"Thanks love."

"Come out of the way of the photographer."

"Come up to the front ma, so everyone can see your nice clothes."

"Daughter, come out of the bloody way."

"Auntie, can me ma come to the front with you?"

I didn't like the way everyone had their photos taken in couples, my mum's partner, Elvid was not invited, and she really stood out being on her own. Mum was constantly made to be photographed standing in the background with her self-conscious and lop sided grin. I tried to protest but mum and the rest of the adults told me to go away and mind my own business. Elvid appeared at some point and it wasn't long before he and my mother became paralytic with drink and began to make a show of themselves.

All eyes were on them as they tried in vain to hold up their heads. Cigarette ash covered the table they sat at as they continually missed the ashtrays in front of them. They could manage with great difficulty to light up a fag, but were unable to smoke it. The silver ash just grew longer and longer waiting to be smoked or stubbed out. I hated Elvid and didn't expect to see him at my beloved brother's big day. I also felt hate for my mother and shame. You bitch, I thought, how could you behave like that on your son's wedding day. Nothing seemed to matter to my mum, nothing seemed important enough for her to stay sober. My mood was becoming bitter when Jimmy appeared at my side.

"Ma's drunk again," I said.

"Don't you worry about your ma, you ok?"

"I'm tired and I wanna go home."

"Don't worry love I'll get somebody to take you."

"Gimme a big kiss. You be a good girl now."

The bride and groom were leaving to go on their honeymoon. I cried uncontrollably as I watched them speed off in Jimmy's white Beetle. The car was covered with good luck messages written in various colours of lipstick. Customary tin cans tied to the car by long pieces of string were dragged along the gravel as they sped off. I was crying because I thought that I was also going on this honeymoon business with them. Instead I was left to go back to the woman who was sprawled across the table barely able to hold her head up, and then I had to try to persuade someone to take us home. You would think that people would offer us a ride home having seen the state my mother was in and as she was supposed to be looking after me. But no, people just seemed to let me get on with it until one of my uncles reluctantly agreed to drop us home. I couldn't understand how people seemed not to notice my grief. The happiness of being an important blue fairy princess was fading and was replaced by the more familiar feeling of invisibility, bad butterflies and anger.

The next day it rained. I stood at the front door silently watching the droplets falling. Soon I was off day dreaming again. Dreaming of how I could get myself a better mummy, dreaming of a better way to dress, to eat, to talk, to live. The rain became heavier with each falling drop and soon it was pouring down. The thunder clapped and I rushed back inside. "See," mum laughed, "God's angry with you." I racked my brains trying to think what I might have done to upset God. I couldn't think of anything bad I'd done recently. "Ma why is God angry with me, I haven't done nuthin." She looked at me with a mischievous twinkle in her eyes, "God sees everything. You must have done something bad whether it was today or yesterday or you might even be thinkin about doin sumthin tomorrow." I vowed to try not to piss God off again and I was scared that he could see everything. With Jimmy gone things at home deteriorated quickly.

Come on Ivy sing that song. She would sit on the hearth at the fireside and close her eyes.

When you lose the one you love,
how lonely life can be
with such a memory ...

Claps and cheers all round for Ivy and another glass of the Tawny wine. She would close her eyes, throw back her head and down the wine with her face screwed up as if she was not enjoying it. She would then glance over at me. She knew I would be watching, waiting for her to get paralytic. Next up was Geordie who yodelled. "Yodel ah de de de , yodel ah de de de." Then we had Laura or Lollipop as we liked to call her, she sang, "my boy lollipop do do do do, ya set my heart on fiya do do do do." No-one ever seemed to finish a whole song, but they all had their favourites.

They sang all night until they were too drunk to hit another note. "Right you bastards," mum slurred, "everybody out, out, get out of my house." They knew not to argue and left. Mum would stagger over to me. "I love you and I love all my children." She'd try to kiss me but the smell of alcohol on her breath disgusted me. The vacant pathetic look in her eyes put me off. I knew now it was time to switch roles and I had to become her mother, put her to bed and make sure my little brothers were ok.

I hated my mother to tell me that she loved me when she was drunk. "How could she love me," I raged. A mother who loves her children would say it all the time. A mother who loved her children would not be in such a state of intoxication. I would somehow get her upstairs to bed, where she would duly piss herself and fall fast asleep. I clung to her urine soaked body. At last, a mummy to hold, to lie next to. Just for a moment, it didn't matter that she was drunk, she was where she should be, beside her children.

I watched her while she slept. Wondered what it would be like to have a normal mummy. I dreamt about it. My normal mummy would not drink; she would think that a disgraceful thing to do. She would be sober, clean and she would look after us properly. She would not beg and scrounge money for the Tawny wine. She would spend that money on food and clothes for us. Food, oh yeah, now I was making myself hungry. I rubbed my belly, scratched my head which was teeming with lice, turned over trying not to burst any of the boils on my arse and cried myself to sleep.

I was often awakened several times in the night by the sound of neighbours fighting or viciously beating their screaming children. More times than I care to remember, those screams were my own as I watched Elvid beating my mother senseless. "You were looking at him weren't you, you nigger loving whore," spat Elvid as he jealously accused mum of flirting. "I haven't done a thing love," mum answered stricken with fear and the knowledge of what was coming next. In seconds Elvid had my mum on the floor kicking her anywhere she failed to shield and punching her face repeatedly with great blows. The screaming, shouting, wailing and shrieking was deafening as we all cried and begged Elvid to leave our mum alone. "Elvid, please don't kill my mummy, please," I begged with all my heart. Elvid wasn't listening, his face was deep red, the veins were visible in his forehead as he pummelled away at what now resembled a rag doll.

I don't remember when it stopped but somehow mum was crawling away and we saw our chance to quickly grab her arms and pull her upstairs to our room. She had pissed herself through fear and she was covered in thick red blood. I felt physically sick as I heard her pitiful groans in the night. Looking down upon her face I could see her pale waxy complexion even in the dark and hear her gasping for breath. The tears spilled out of my eyes in desperation and fear. Elvid was next door and I could hear his massive body throwing itself across the bed. I was petrified in case he came back in for more. I lay very still and softened the noise of mum's groans with my hand held gently over her mouth, then snoring ... I couldn't sleep until I heard that monster snoring, the fear wouldn't let me. I always slept deeply after crying, it was a relief from the exhaustion of the terrifying scenes around me. The sounds of other neighbours crying out in pain were muffled, and the morning came more quickly.

The next morning the beast had gone off to work when we woke up.

"Oh, dear God. Get me a neck tie or a belt daughter," mum whispered.

"Here, take this ma." I handed her a belt.

"Help me love. Tie it real tight around my chest."

"Oh, gently, gently, don't hurt mummy."

As she nursed her broken ribs and gingerly edged her way out of the bed, I could see the full extent of Elvid's wrath.

My mum's body looked broken and she had two black eyes. "Get me the dark glasses love before you go to school," she panted. When the neighbours saw mum that morning, they just shook their heads. Nobody stretched out their warm loving arms to cuddle us or ask us if we were ok. Nobody questioned what had happened because they knew. They knew what had happened in our house the night before because the walls were paper thin, because you would have to be deaf not to hear our pleas for help and our agonising screams as we watched our mother being slaughtered in front of us. No, everything was accepted as normal for Ivy and her wee darkies. This was our normal life where no-one questioned the screams the night before or the belt around mum's rib cage and I was quite sure they didn't think she was wearing dark glasses because maybe she'd turned into a fucking superstar overnight.

I could hardly speak, hoarse from crying and screaming.

My eyes were red and puffy and I had a bad headache, but I was happier in the mornings because I could go to school and see normal people and do normal things. If I could get myself to school, I had a routine, food to eat and I could play with my friends. We didn't even have a clock, but I had trained myself to guess the time and I was rarely late to school. I was even called on by other neighbours to wake them, like a human alarm clock. I had help from the town clock housed inside St Mark's Church which stood proudly just across the road from Market Street. I would listen anxiously for the hammer of the clock to strike eight, boom, boom, boom, it clanged. My anxiety got the better of me. Had I missed a boom? I jumped up out of bed clutching my heart which was thundering with palpitations brought on by the thought I might be late for school.

Most of the children in my street attended Edenderry Primary School, a big gloomy yellow brick building on Carrickblacker Road. Unnervingly, the head teacher's accommodation was situated next to the school. It had cold dark toilets out in the yard with harsh plastic-like paper to wipe your arse on. I wasn't very bright at primary school. It was hard to concentrate when you didn't get proper nutritious food to eat, when you didn't get to sleep much before three in the morning, when you spent most nights being totally traumatised by witnessing scenes of violence ending with your mother being beaten to within an inch of her life and my brothers and I begging for her mercy, when you were plagued with boils on your bottom, worms up your bottom and head lice. I tickled and hurt everywhere, there was no respite. The hurt was not just physical pain it was mental too.

Even at such a tender young age, I was mortified and embarrassed beyond belief that my person was crawling with bugs and covered in unsightly lesions. Once I was trying to read a book in class, when my forehead began to tickle. I felt the usual compulsion to scratch my head with the venom of a dog with distemper. I broke out in a sweat when I looked down and there before me lay a huge brown louse. I quickly killed it on the book leaving a bloody great stain on the page. I nervously looked around the room, had anyone seen me. I was ashamed of the state my body was in and sad and angry with my mother who didn't, couldn't or wouldn't do anything about it. In school I always sat by the window, where the sun warmed me. I loved the heat, I was like an iguana, soaking it up and doing my daydreaming about a different way of living.

Chapter Four

Poverty

"Is Annie comin out to play?" asked Shirley, one of Lollipop's daughters. Shirley had a beautiful face and a full head of blonde curly hair.

"Come on Annie they're playing skipin over there," shouted Shirley taking me by my hand.

"Fuck off, she can't play because she's a darkie."

"No I'm not," I stuttered, "I'm a Protestant."

"Fuck off you're not allowed to play this game."

I ran off into my house in tears angry and confused.

"Mum, they won't let me play because they said I'm a darkie," I yelled.

"Stop cryin and go and tell them you're a Protestant and they're to let you play before I go out there."

"See, told you I was a Protestant," I gleefully told them.

"I'm a Protestant and my ma says you're to let me play before she has to come out."

"Oh, she is a Protestant! Ok, come on then."

This is what I had to go through every day when I wanted to join in with the children playing out in the street. One day they'd say I was too black, the next day, too small, the next day my hair was too curly, the next day they thought I wasn't a real Protestant. It was all very tiring and it made me very angry that every single day someone somewhere wanted to hate me for something or exclude me for reasons I couldn't understand. I was determined not to be left out and I wouldn't give up, I couldn't. If I gave up, that would be that and I would never play again. I wished that everyone would get off my back, let me breathe, let me come out and play without being questioned. I was just plain wee Annie who wanted to skip rope or play hopscotch like all the other children.

"Annie," mum shouted in her angry voice. "I want you to take that washin down to the launderette." I hated taking down the laundry. Mum always made me carry so much and I could hardly see over the big bag when crossing the road. "Alan will take the other bags down but you go on ahead of him now." I picked up the black bin liner full to the brim with sour smelling clothes. I reached the half way mark that was the zebra crossing on the corner of the street where the fenians got their heads kicked in coming home from work. The hood of my coat was up hiding my uncombed afro and I had trouble looking right and left. Somehow, I managed to stagger all the way to the launderette without dropping the bag or getting killed by a passing car.

The launderette smelt clean and it was lovely and warm. I found an empty machine and began to load it. Alan appeared with a face like a smacked arse and began loading two other machines close by. We placed some coins in the slots and the machines clicked into action. Alan said he was off to play a quick game of football and warned that I had better call him the minute the machines stopped. "Annie," shouted Fay who managed the launderette. She was shaking me by my shoulders and her face was so close to mine that I could smell her stinking breath. I had fallen asleep sitting by a window that let in the sun. The sound of the machines had rocked me into a slumber and I was so warm and cosy. I quickly jumped up to escape any further onslaught of the breath.

"I thought I told you to call me when they finished," Alan scolded angrily. "I'm sorry, I fell asleep," I replied. We began to put the clothes into some empty dryers. This was the bit I loved because I liked to taunt my brother. "What machine shall I put this in?" I asked loudly and with mock innocence as I slowly and deliberately held up one of mum's bras for Alan's attention. "Put that down you wee bitch," he laughed. "Oh, and where should these go?" I continued with a pair of mum's knickers held above my head. We fell about laughing hysterically. Eventually we had stuffed all the clothes into several dryers. Fay appeared and with an angry grimace reminded us that, "you can't put so much into each dryer, do you want to break them?" Mum had warned us to use the dryers sparingly in case she could get some money back. "It's alright Fay the machines won't break," we protested. "Take them out and spread them into at least one other dryer right now," she demanded. We did as she asked with a, "Fuckin bitch," under our breath. Alan ran off to finish his game.

"Is Alan your brother?" enquired Fay.

"Yeah."

"So who is Jimmy then?"

"He's my brother too."

"He can't be your brother, he's white," she laughed.

"He is my brother."

"No, he's not. He's probably your uncle."

"Fay, he is my brother," I insisted.

"Oh, perhaps he's your half-brother."

I didn't know what a half-brother meant. Fay made me really mad and I was a little confused. I had never questioned Jimmy's relationship to me. I was sure he was my brother even if he was white.

"Ma, is Jimmy my brother?" I asked returning with the clean clothes.

"Yes, he's your brother why?"

"Cos Fay says he can't be, he's white"

"What the fuck does that nosey bitch know? What an interferin evil auld cow."

"She says he's my uncle."

"Well he's your brother and it's none of her business what colour he is."

"Ma will you tell Fay that when you see her?"

"I'll tell her about her pasty face, her filthy house and her drunken bastard of a husband, that's what I'll tell her." I think my mother was more than a little upset that Fay had asked me personal questions about my family relationships and I thought, God help Fay if my ma bumps into her anytime soon, especially if she's drunk.

It was Sunday morning and I was very excited. Having just done the laundry recently, I know I put it here somewhere. I searched high and low for my best dress. The one my granddad had bought me for my birthday. It was white with little blue flowers and a dark blue ribbon in the middle. My mum never bought me a birthday card or present in my whole life so the dress had a special significance to me. I had hardly slept because I was too excited. My mum, the best mum in the world really did love me. She had promised to take us to the seaside. The town clock boomed eight times and I was up before the eighth strike. I'd run a damp cloth over my teeth and my face and everything. My little brothers were standing next to me, smelling of green fairy soap and waiting to be inspected for some form of cleanliness. I kissed and squeezed them with pride, "are you ready," I whispered. They smiled up at me with those big brown eyes. Us, the Yella's, going to the seaside. I called to her, "Mummy, where's my summer dress?" no answer. I didn't want to annoy her so I quickly put on my orange dress, a hand me down from a well-meaning neighbour. It was velvet with long sleeves and a little draw string in the middle. It was jaded, too short and too late! My long arms dangled awkwardly from the sleeves that ended two inches above my wrists.

"Mum, are you ready?"

"Ready for what?" she roared.

"The seaside mum."

"I have no money for the seaside."

"But mum you said you would take us."

"I say a lot of things," she threw back at me. She had that familiar look on her face. The one that told me, I was drunk last night and didn't really mean it.

The penny finally dropped and I guessed that she'd sold my precious dress for the Tawny wine. Later that day I found out that mum had torn up my dress and used it to clean the windows. "It was too short for you anyway now quit snivelling." The same day, I found out that she'd given my gold bracelet to one of our neighbours, the one that Jimmy bought me. The tears came easily, burning my cheeks. "Don't cry sis," said Gabriel as he hugged me close. "When I grow up I'm gonna buy you loads of nice things." No seaside, why did she always do this to me, does she not know that I believe her lies. Does she not know that it breaks my little heart when I find out that I'm not going to the seaside?

I saw the look on my little brothers faces, I could have killed my mother for putting that look there. I felt worthless and crushed inside. They were my things and she'd taken it upon herself to get rid of them, just like that, for the wine that she was now throwing up into the toilet. "You bitch," I spat, "I wish I had a real mummy, I hate you." I stormed out into the street, into Florence Court. Everything seemed normal outside. Kids were playing hopscotch, football, parents were fighting and dogs were scratching around in the dirt. Some kids were singing,

> Eenie meenie minee mo
> catch a nigger by the toe
> when he squeals let him go
> eenie meenie minee mo.

Everyone laughed and pointed at us. My brothers stood there looking lost, dirty and sad. Yes, everything was normal. I hated the person who wrote that song, it hurt. How could anyone get away with making up a song that hurt the feelings of little black children? We are humans too, we feel things, we do cry too when we hurt. Years later I learned the actual words of the song were, catch a 'piggy' by the toe ... bastards.

Gabriel had an idea to cheer us all up. Even if we couldn't go to the seaside we could pretend. We spent the rest of the morning doing something that we did often, looking at an old catalogue of household items and clothing. We called it the 'club book' because mum said you had to join a club to pay for the items weekly.

"When I grow up I'm having everything on that page," I gushed.

"No, I want the ironing board," my brother cried.

"Oh alright then, have it," I agreed.

We really believed that these things were ours. I remember the feeling of excitement, thinking that I might one day own a proper doll or a hairdryer or even a coal shuttle. You had to agree to take whatever was on a whole page, so you didn't always get what you wanted. You could swap your 'presents' with someone else, and we were always generous with each other. Who would have thought that in later life, this simple 'game' would help me to establish a flair for fashion, interior decorating and living well for less.

Granddad was great, he was always bailing us out. Like the day I ran to him crying that mum wouldn't give me money to have a haircut. The 'Shag' was in thanks to the likes of rock chic, Suzi Quatro, David Cassidy and The Bay City Rollers. The Shag was a layered cut and looked best with shorter hair. Just about all the older girls in my street appeared with a shaggy haircut overnight. It was all the rage and all they talked about. They walked about the street combing their hair at regular intervals in case you didn't notice the Shag. I was envious and as always, I didn't want to be left out. I was aware of my growing afro and asked my friends if they thought I too could have the Shag. They firmly assured me that indeed I could and that I should do so immediately.

My mother laughed and tried to explain the Shag wouldn't work for my type of barnet. She reminded me about the times I'd gone to the local hairdressers in the past just for a trim. We fell about laughing as I recalled one occasion where my afro had reached new heights that would put the whole of the Jackson family combined to shame. As I neared the salon I could see the hairdressers craning their necks. On entering the shop, it appeared empty inside. I was confused when the manager told me there was nobody available today. Then I heard the nervous laughter from the back room. It dawned on me they were hiding. That's when I became aware of the skill necessary in taming my tresses, and sadly, these ladies were only used to blue rinses, backcombing and cutting straight hair. After this incident, I was regularly turned away with all manner of excuses. On the rare occasions one of the stylists (I use the word lightly) relented. This was mainly because I'd taken to hanging outside the shop peering in waiting to catch them coming out of the back room. It must have been quite a shock to see a black face squashed up against the window with an afro resembling a piper's busby. They jumped a fair few feet when they clocked me, peeping.

"Alright don't cry dear, I can cut your hair for you."

Granddad took me into his house, held me between his legs like I'd watched him do with his dogs and promptly gave me a short back and sides using the dogs grooming shears. It looked absolutely nothing like the Shag, but a girl can dream, and you know how I liked to dream. Somehow, I pretended I had the Shag, although I couldn't quite get the comb through my hair with the ease the other girls did. Anyway, I was looking forward to showing off my new hair cut in school. Granddad used to buy all our school uniforms and he made sure we had two of everything. I was showing off trying, and failing, to flick my hair the way I'd seen the other girls do, when my friend casually commented she wasn't able to get the Shag until next week because her mother needed the money to wash her uniform. I was amazed at this because I couldn't remember seeing my mother laundering our uniforms. She washed our shirts and socks but trousers and tunics, no, I don't recall the washing of those items except in the school half term time.

"What? You mean you have your uniform washed before Christmas?"

"I have my uniform washed every week you cheeky bitch," my friend laughed.

I thought that greyish shine was my uniform sparkling, I didn't realise it was ground in dirt. It was a good job our tunics were black. I was too ashamed to admit that our uniforms were not washed often and nervously joined in with a false laugh pretending I was joking. I began to dwell on this washing of uniforms every week, "God," I thought, "ours must be filthy." I was embarrassed and after school I marched into my house to demand to know why our uniforms weren't washed every week.

"Where do you think I would get the money to wash your uniforms every week, do you think I'm Rockefeller?" She pronounced that, Rackafella.

"But Didi says hers gets washed every week."

"Fuck off down to Fay and ask her if she'll wash it for free, and pay for my gas," mum scoffed.

Mum sent me back outside with a warm ear for my troubles. I held my ear for a moment to caress the pain out of it and shrugged, it was my fault. I shouldn't have approached her when we didn't even have money for the gas meter. Usually when the 'meter man' visited he would greet my mother with a knowing look. He knew he was about to make a discovery of skulduggery. The same skulduggery he had likely discovered on a regular basis in most of the homes in my street. He stacked the coins up in little piles, sorting through them to take what was owed and give my mother back all the filed down coins she used to dupe the meter into giving up free gas. Like others in the street, my mother was good at filing down coins to fit the meter slot in her efforts to survive poverty whilst feeding her drinking habit.

Granddad would have our electricity re-connected when we got cut off, as we often did when mum had gone a bit mad with the drinking and couldn't pay those bills either. As children, we sometimes found not having electricity exciting. Mum would light candles and we'd sit watching the shadows on the walls, as the flames flickered this way and that. "Look that shadow looks like a goat, that one like a cloud and that one like a . . ." The shadow game made us sleepy in a natural and pleasant way, which was probably healthier than the sleep brought on by the lilac liquid or the lash of a belt.

Granddad fed us when we were hungry and generally took Jimmy's place in acting like a father figure. I started to call him "da," as that's what everyone else called their daddies. I knew he wasn't my father but I used to get jealous of other children when they spoke of their "da's." I wanted to know what it was like to call someone "da" and as I had no "da" my granddad was the next best thing. I couldn't imagine what it was like to have a real da. From my observations, they seemed to be the bosses of all the houses and the women and they always spoiled anything that was considered fun. This had a profound effect on me in later adulthood. I could be having the most fun in a friend's house, but the moment the father figure returned I'd be out the door in a flash. I always dodged my friend's questioning of this. But deep down I had an irresistible urge to run away from all dads, I just didn't feel comfortable around them.

I had long since forgotten my own father and what he looked like. I remember vaguely, one time my mother took me to see my father after they had separated for some considerable time. I'd not seen another black person outside of my family and was accustomed to being around white people only. My father, a very dark skinned man, stood waiting for us as we disembarked at Liverpool docks. As we approached, he smiled widely exposing his yellow stained teeth. My mother picked me up and pushed me into his open arms. This stranger began hugging me tightly and to his amusement, I went berserk. My father laughed as I kicked, and scratched wildly at him until he couldn't hold me and had to put me down. My heart was thumping and I couldn't believe my mother would just plonk me in his arms like that. She was a little embarrassed as I clung tightly to her legs shaking with anger and fear. My father mumbled something like, 'She's a little fighter isn't she.' I think having been a boxer, my father was proud that I too had the killer instinct.

When granddad took me into town for a walk, I studied the colour of my little brown hand in his. I would steal glances at him, trying to work out whether he was ashamed of walking in the streets with his black grandchild. I was beginning to develop a sense of awareness of black and white skins. This observation was encouraged by the ignorant people around me reminding me of my difference every single day. I was becoming aware of how different I was from my friends and even other members of my family. I was frustrated about how some viewed my blackness. "It's not her fault, it's the way she was born," some would offer as if it was an affliction, by way of explaining my colour to others who questioned.

When I cried after being taunted about the colour of my skin, well-meaning neighbours would try to comfort me by saying, 'You tell them you're a lovely chocolate drop'. I wasn't comforted, I was screaming with rage inside. I wasn't a chocolate anything, just a human being. Their ignorance was so overwhelmingly suffocating and I didn't know how to educate them or how to make them stop. My low self-esteem grew steadily, creeping up on me and hanging on. Like the bad butterflies, I couldn't control those horrible feelings. They made me feel worthless, frightened and angry. I held my granddad's hand tighter trying to reassure myself I was loved and I couldn't find any signs to tell me he minded being seen with me. It must have been a bit of a dilemma for those I grew up with, trying to reconcile learned feelings of hate for the colour of our skin with their more instinctive feelings of like or love for us as people they had a relationship with, as relatives or just neighbours.

I hated being referred to as "that wee darkie." I hated the way white people patted my head and stroked my hair as if I were a dog. I hated the way they examined me and touched my skin to see if it would come off. I felt constantly violated. When they made comments about 'those niggers' and I squared up to them in confrontation, they tried to quieten me with 'not you, you're one of us'. I didn't look like one of them, I didn't feel like one of them, they didn't treat me like one of them and I didn't want to be like them. I didn't view the world the way they did. I didn't want to hate people for any reason and I certainly didn't want to kill anyone for being different. Yet, I was surrounded by people who were killing those that did look like them, people who were one of them, friends, neighbours, relatives and acquaintances. That was a very confusing and scary thought. Clearly the learned hatred of someone's religion could not be reconciled with any earlier like or love of that person as a human being and neighbour.

I sat pondering in silence on the window sill at the front of the house. "What's the matter Annie," enquired my friend and next door neighbour Roda.

"Oh I'm kinda sick of being black and I would like to get it off," I replied innocently.

"Oh, you want it off."

"Can you get it off me then?"

"No problem. Come on over to my house and I'll help you to get it off."

I was so excited and followed eagerly. Just like that I was gonna get it off and be white and happy all at the same time! Why didn't we think of this before, I wondered? Roda put some hot water in a big red bowl. Next, she added a big dollop of bleach and told me, "Right, roll your sleeves up." She then got out a well-used scrubbing brush that was used to remove stains from clothes and for scrubbing clean the front step. She began scrubbing with all her might.

"Ouch, you're hurting me."

"Don't worry its coming off."

"Ouch, it hurts, it hurts."

"Maybe we need more bleach, but my ma will kill me."

"Look, my arms are red."

"Sorry Annie, we'll try again later."

My arms stung and were swollen and red. Fuck this for a lark, I thought, it's too painful trying to get it off and somehow, I knew it was going to be more painful keeping it on. I'll try again tomorrow, I concluded. It was hard trying to be black and be a Protestant at the same time. There were so many rules I didn't understand, so many 'Orange' songs I had to learn the words to and I didn't even understand what I was singing about! The marching season took place every twelfth and thirteenth of July. The streets were crammed full of various loyalist bands laying claim to their streets. The flutes and drums beat out familiar Protestant tunes.

> Sure it's old but it is beautiful
> And its colours they are fine
> It was worn at Derry, Augherin
> Enniskillen and the Boyne
> Sure my father wore it when a youth
> In bygone days of yore
> And it's on the twelfth I love to wear
> The sash my father wore.

I silently cursed my mother for bringing me into such a cruel world. I didn't want to sing these stupid songs, I didn't want to be a Protestant and I didn't want to hear those drums anymore. I wasn't meant to be born black and poor, I raged. Damn you mum, damn you.

"Why do I have to go?" I asked sulkily when mum demanded that I go to the shop for her. My mother didn't understand the root of my reluctance. Anytime I had to leave our street was like trying to complete an assault course. On a regular basis, I had to dodge vicious free roaming dogs, vicious free roaming neighbours, lurking strangers, suspected paedophiles, flashers, drunks and people clearly mentally ill. As soon as I stepped out of the house Buddy, my next-door neighbour's dog, rounded on me. Buddy was an old black and white cross breed who looked like a fat sheep. He was scruffy and always angry. I nervously crossed to the other side of the street, watching him to make sure he didn't jump up to bite me. Good dog, good dog, I whispered. The bad butterflies woke up because they could sense some drama about to unfold and they didn't want to miss that. Buddy made a run for me, then quickly turned away. I swear that beast had a grin on his face as if to say, 'Gotcha!' It was as though he just had to show you he was still capable of scaring the shit out of you despite being old and fat.

As I turned the corner, the bad butterflies circled my stomach expectantly. Bad butterflies featured heavily in my life. Sometimes they came just to fuck about with me, sometimes to warn me of danger and sometimes to force me to act! They didn't tell me how to act, just that I should do something. The door just had to be open. I saw him standing in the shadows of his hallway, just visible enough to ensure the fear of God would be instilled in me as I passed. He made a sound like that of a wailing ghost but to my relief, he stayed where he was. I was relieved that I could get past Gordon's house without incident. Normally he would try to spit on me and call me names as I passed his house. "Hello wee fuckin niggy noggy," he'd squeal with delight as I passed. I couldn't work out why Gordon made it his duty to watch me and my movements. It was unnerving and I soon found out he was not the only one watching. I wondered who else might be lurking behind those curtains.

At the top of the street were the vigilantes sitting behind a make shift barricade that stretched across the whole road. Hi, I said to the three men on 'duty'. They nodded and Neville, who knew my brother Alan said, 'Oh hello love' cheerily. At last I reached the corner shop, with a feeling of relief, but that was short lived. As I stood waiting for my bread and eggs I became aware of someone behind me. "Hello little girl," said a man in a slick grey suit and sporting a brown pock marked face. I didn't know this Indian man but he seemed to be in the shop a lot when I was there. I shifted uneasily from one foot to the other and didn't answer him.

Albert, the shopkeeper entered with the eggs that he'd gone to get from the back of the store. "Would you like some sweeties?" asked the Indian man in a strange accent. I shook my head and the man insisted, "Come on darling, what would you like, I'm not going to hurt you." I looked to Albert for comfort and he told the Indian man, "It's alright mate, the wee girl doesn't want no sweets. Her ma wouldn't let her take sweets from strangers anyhow." I thought, "that's a lie." The Indian man said, "But we're not strangers are we dear, I see you in here all the time, don't I?"

Albert told the man that if he insisted on buying me some sweets he should do so and leave them on the counter for me. He chose a big packet of glacier fruits. When he left the shop, Albert put the sweets in my hand and told me, "Get off home to your mummy now and don't you stop to talk to that man if he's outside. Do you hear me Annie?" I nodded that I did hear him. I was nervous about the fact that the man might be waiting for me. As I stepped outside I noticed a big black car suspiciously parked across the road. I began running as fast as I could when I realised he was watching me from a half open window. I knew he wouldn't dare to follow me past the vigilantes because he was not from around our area and if he tried to enter my streets, that might be the last time he ever watched me or any other child again.

There were vigilantes at every street corner, so no stranger could enter the street without being noticed and checked out. You'd better be a Protestant if you came to our street or you might find yourself in 'Romper Room.' This was a room used by the paramilitary, where organised beatings took place. It was named after a children's educational television programme where children played safely in a big bright room as they learned lessons whilst having fun. They happily sang . . .

I always do what's right
I never do anything wrong
I'm a Romper Room baby
A baby all day long

Unfortunately, for any poor unknown beggar who entered Florence Court's Romper Room, their playing days were over and they were taught a very different lesson. For those who were known, criminal activities were not permitted to be carried out without the UDA's permission. Anyone who failed to obey this rule could be severely beaten or worse, knee capped. The latter involved a bullet being fired into the back of the legs and was meant to cripple the victim as a warning. This was a regular form of punishment used in Ulster throughout the 'troubles'. As curious, innocent children, we would wait until we thought no-one was around before sneaking in to the Romper Room house to have a look at the blood-stained walls, after a punishment had taken place. Today, I hurried past trying not to look in the window for fear that someone might be in there dying from a beating or a shooting.

Just as I was passing Gordon's house on my return, I looked to my right and saw Nick and his brother Ewan. They called me over to where they were standing. Shirley joined us and we ate the sweets whilst I told them about the Indian man. "I'd better get these things up to my ma," I said, making to leave. Ewan put his foot out as if to try and trip me up, "Where do you think you're goin?" he asked. "I just said I need to go to my ma." The brothers were up to something and began whispering and laughing. "See that puddle;" said Nick, "I want you both to drink some water from it. If you don't do it, you're not goin any fuckin where and we'll take the rest of your sweets."

Shirley and I looked at each other, then the puddle and I began to hatch a plan of action. I decided that I was going to pretend to drink the water in the hope they would feel sorry for me not knowing I was acting, just to get away. As I knelt towards the puddle Ewan suddenly shouted, "No, it's ok, you can go." This is just what I had hoped for, one or the other taking pity on me. I couldn't believe that my act had worked and I was free to go. Poor Shirley was not so lucky. As I made my way up the hill towards my house I looked back and shouted, "Suckers. I wasn't gonna drink the water anyway." Shirley escaped as the brothers' attention was now on me. Ewan tried to catch up with me but I was too fast.

Determined to make sure he was no sucker he grabbed a stick and smeared it with green shit left by the rag and bone man's donkey earlier. Ewan flung the shit as hard as he could in my direction and to my horror a big blob landed on my shoulder. I was disgusted as the whiff of the shit found its way up my nostrils. Ewan and Nick were ecstatic and high fived each other. "What the fuck?" began mum as I stumbled inside the house. When I'd finished telling my mum about Ewan and Nick's antics she marched off to enlighten their parents. I felt warm and happy when I heard their yelps a little later as their mum lashed the belt down on their legs. I high fived my tiny tears dolly. Because I'd been so traumatised my mum let me have a tea party on the pavement outside my front door. I gathered up my red plastic cups, saucers and tea pot and arranged them on the ground. I tipped up the tea pot pouring a cup of orange juice for my dolly and we chatted away the afternoon. Oh, 'twas bliss.

Christmas was nearing and my mum was sad. She didn't have any money to buy us anything. "Annie, are you coming with me to visit the cruelty man love?" asked my mum. I didn't like going to the cruelty man's house because it made me feel like we were begging, which we were. The cruelty man was a local welfare officer who was well aware of us and our circumstances. He visited homes on our street bringing second hand toys for the kids sometimes. My granddad threatened my mum with the cruelty man a lot and said he would come and take us away.

"So, what are you getting for Christmas Annie?" asked a nosey neighbour. I didn't answer, but I was sure it would be something really special because my mum had promised, "Honest to God" she would stop drinking and make sure we had the best Christmas ever. Mum was drunk on Christmas Eve and as she sat on the sofa I approached her. "Ma, what are we getting for Christmas?" She didn't answer. I was angry and I began to cry. "I bet you haven't gotten us anything, have you, have you?" I looked at my little brothers and felt sorry for them. It was Christmas tomorrow and not a present in sight. I had an idea and shared it with Gabriel. "Yeah, good idea sis at least it's something," he said cheerfully.

We carefully wrapped up some old toys that mum had gotten from the 'cruelty man' recently. They were mostly broken, but we felt they would do and at least we'd have something to open on Christmas Day. When my granddad came to visit on Christmas Day he had a fit. "You old witch," he shouted at my mother. "How could you let your wee children be without presents or food on Christmas Day?" He walked out in disgust slamming the door behind him. Mum began to cry then we all joined in. As we tucked into some bread and butter my grandfather reappeared at the door. I could see that my uncles were behind him. He took my mum into the hall and we heard him angrily telling her what a bad mother she was. "You're no good Ivy and I will call the cruelty man if I have to. Do you understand me?" Mum nodded and dried her eyes.

Granddad said he would bring his Christmas food up to our house for mum to cook and we would all eat together. They had even scraped up some presents for us. I opened mine and shrieked with glee. It was a cardboard doll. She came with clothes that had to be cut out from sheets of paper to be hung on her fragile body. My little brothers had some green plastic soldiers and some marbles. We had great fun playing 'knock down soldier'. The tiny green figures were lined up in the hallway and we took turns in killing them off one by one, flicking the big marbles to knock them over. There were a few toy cars and Billy happily sucked on the car wheels dribbling and giggling between mouthfuls of mashed potato. The adults watched us and smiled but no-one spoke to my mother.

Sometimes I was sad when granddad threatened my mother with the cruelty man. She looked like a broken little girl being scolded. I think he said it in desperation and to shake her up, shake some motherly love into her and some responsibility. It didn't work though. It was the same with her drinking, I was always exhausting myself, trying to make her stop, but she just didn't seem able. The previous Christmas was different.

I got my coat and followed mum. We walked a long way and it was very cold. The cruelty man lived in a huge period house and the pebbles on the way up to his front door crunched under our feet as we walked. Mum thumped the big brass door knocker. "Awk Ivy how are ye doin. Come in, come in," he said cheerily. "Hello again, Annie, is it?" I smiled and nodded. Mum started acting all different, like she had manners and grace. My nose was running and she took out her hankie and gently wiped the snot away. I rolled my eyes thinking, "Oh not using the end of your sleeve like you normally do then?" We had tea from little bone china cups with matching saucers. As soon as I began sipping the scalding liquid, the flesh on the roof of my mouth and tongue came loose. I dared not wince as I knew what the consequences would be. Mum had warned me earlier to refuse everything offered.

Mum was offered a biscuit, "Oh no thank you we've just eaten," she lied. I was offered bread and jam but refused it politely, shaking my head as I couldn't speak with the pain and loose skin. My mum had always warned us that when we were visiting we were not allowed to take any food. Mum said people might think we were hungry bastards or that she didn't feed us properly. I was so hungry and I felt tortured as the cruelty man left the biscuits and sandwiches on the table in front of us. I wondered if he would notice me slipping one or two down the sides of my socks, but decided against it. My mum saw my eyes widening and my mouth frothing. Sensing that I wouldn't be able to hold out much longer, she quickly got down to the business of telling him about our woes. Before ushering us out into the cold he gave mum some second-hand clothes and toys for us and informed her that we were eligible to attend a Christmas party that was being hosted by the British army.

My little brothers whooped with delight. We'd never been to a proper party in our lives. On the Saturday morning mum stuck to her side of the bargain and had us up and dressed before nine. I felt special in my recently acquired second hand clothes and second hand shoes. They were a little tight for me but my mum said no-one would notice and it was only for the day. When we reached the hall where the party was to take place we were astonished to find our names on little cards on the table. A soldier who introduced himself as Jason came up to me and said, "Hello my lovely. Can you find your name?" I was shocked that Jason was black. I'd never seen another person who looked like me outside of my family except on TV. The bad butterflies came but they gave me good tickles in my tummy, I wasn't expecting that! I studied Jason discreetly, he was very loud and jolly and for a moment I felt good about myself.

Somehow, I felt connected to Jason. I could tell that he was not having low self-esteem issues like me. I wanted to know more about him but I knew it would seem odd to just blurt out the many questions I had. I wanted to know where he came from, how he managed to act so normal, why was he being so kind to me and who brushed his hair. I stopped myself from popping down day dream alley as he pointed to the piece of card that said Annie. Jason pulled out my chair to let me sit down. I was a little cautious because the only time anyone had ever previously pulled out a chair for me, was to make sure I didn't notice and fell flat on my arse. But not Jason, no, he tucked me under the table and asked if I was comfortable. I'd never sat at a proper table before and I lied that I was. Jason could tell by my expression and the awkward way I was slumped, that I was not as comfortable as I could be. He gently helped me to sit up straight and pushed me nearer so I could reach the cutlery on the table.

I was a little anxious that my brothers weren't next to me

but Jason told me not to worry and that it was a great way to meet other children and make friends. I was out of my comfort zone; Jason obviously didn't know that other children shied away from us because we were 'different'. I lifted my head and looked around the table for the first time. Everyone seemed to be looking at me. I was immediately paralysed by self-consciousness. The butterflies circled and threatened and I felt tearful and sick. FUCK OFF! I thought I'd shouted that out loud, but thankfully, it turned out I said it in my head. The self-doubt, the butterflies, the staring faces, were not going to get the better of me today. I said it again in my head, FUCK OFF! I felt the butterflies scattering from my wrath and my stomach began to settle. The other children and their parents continued to watch us curiously but it wasn't long before we were all chatting and joining in the various games. Making new friends did not come easy to me. I was always on my guard, waiting for the rejection, the remarks about my different skin colour, to be interrupted like I didn't exist and that what I had to say wasn't important.

At first I didn't know how to join in the games when invited, because I always had to fight to join in with my friends. I forced myself to accept the friendship these strangers offered and gradually I began to relax. I became excited as I could smell the food. Jason and his friends began serving it up. We had turkey, ham, bacon rolled into little logs, roast potatoes, little sausages, stuffing and all kinds of vegetables. My plate was overflowing and although there's no denying I was a hungry child, I couldn't finish everything on my plate. We had trifle and custard to finish.

It was to be the best Christmas I would ever enjoy as a

child. I had really enjoyed the day playing with the new children, having such lovely food and seeing my mum sober for almost a whole day albeit there was not a drop of alcohol in sight. Just as I thought we were getting ready to go home Jason popped his head around the door and shouted, "Are you all ready to meet Santa?" The children screamed with delight and we followed him outside. When we had all been gathered in the garden Jason told us to look up in the air. A helicopter appeared and we all started cheering and waving as we could see Santa inside.

The helicopter landed close to us. The noise of the whirring blades was deafening and I was frightened that they might fly off and knock me dead. As Santa stepped out the cheers grew louder. We could see a huge red sack with white fur around the rim and Santa was having some difficulty dragging it from the aircraft. Santa told us to line up because he had presents for us. I waited patiently for my name and when he called me I had a smile from one ear to the other. "Ho ho ho. Have you been a good girl?" I nodded and grabbed the present as fast and as politely as I could. I hadn't actually been good, but didn't everyone lie to Santa? The mystery was beautifully wrapped in colourful paper that had my name on it. Santa was reluctant to let go and warned, "Now don't open this until Christmas Day ok?"

That party had a good effect on me. I felt good about myself for a whole day and although the bad butterflies threatened me, they didn't hang around like they usually did. I met and played with strangers who didn't push me away, I ate proper food, I was given presents, my brothers were happy, my mother was sober and I met a wonderful black man, Jason. He made me feel normal and proud of myself. That day a little seed was planted in my head and in my heart and I thought I'd tasted normality. It tasted good, just like I'd dreamed. I had to start to believe in me and concentrate on myself, somehow try and filter out the 'white noise' so I could breathe. I couldn't resist the temptation to do a little day dreaming about finding a better life where I could feel like I felt today. Maybe even one day I could escape Ireland and run away like my mother had done. I was becoming confused about the butterflies because today even they were my friends and I think they hugged me!

Chapter Five

Fun at the Dump

"Coming to the dump?" my brother Gabriel asked. I followed him without answering. Wade's pottery factory in Watson Street was around the corner from our house. The factory was built on the site of an old linen mill and initially produced ceramics for the electricity supply industry and the post office. A quick look around to ensure there was no-one about, and we leapt over the wall into the field where the tip lay. Jumping the wall was not as easy as it sounds, beyond the wall and in several places, were thick nettle patches. Huge green lively stinging nettles around four feet tall. We used to copy the older children and practice climbing up that wall. The older kids could scale the wall easily and in one movement turn around to sit down. They seemed oblivious to the nettles. I was in awe, watching them playfully shoving one another around without a care for the stingers. After several awkward attempts and finally successfully scaling the wall, I tried to pretend that I didn't care about the nettles. Amongst these children were those who had regularly tried to drown me at the swimming pool, so I was aware of the consequences of showing fear.

Before long there was little room left on the wall and one of my younger friends, Mavis, showed up. She was so small and beautiful with blonde wavy hair and big blue innocent eyes. She had no chance of scaling that wall. The older boys grabbed her hands and pulled her up on to the wall. I didn't think that was a good idea, but I kept quiet through fear. Mavis began rocking back and forth and I had palpitations. No-one else seemed to notice as they were lost in ribbing each other and telling jokes. Suddenly Mavis disappeared and only her screams alerted others that she had fallen backwards right in to the middle of a thick nettle patch. Arms flailed everywhere as the older kids tried to get her out. I will never forget the sight of that little girl's body when she was rescued. Her pale white body was covered in huge red wheals, where the nettles had clawed and tore her delicate skin. Her lips were blue and her body was stiff with shock as she was carted off to hospital.

We dug out the ornaments that had been dumped on death row because some big know it all at Wades considered them to be 'seconds' or imperfect. We used our bare hands to dig out the beautiful pieces of pottery. One man's rubbish is another man's treasure. Nothing was a 'second' or imperfect to us. The broken fragments clawed at the skin on our hands and legs, scratching us and sometimes drawing blood. But we were too intent on making some money to worry about a lost pint of blood or two. My brother Gabriel was a champion at digging out all the best pieces. At times this caused friction, as the older boys would try to take his haul. Gabriel could not be caught easily and was fast on his feet. He had learned the art of sprinting and reacting in a split second to escape his own dangerous and daily assault course. He could scale most walls like spider man, faster than most. He liked to scale the walls at the back of our house and along the alley. Gabriel would be in stitches telling us how he would frighten the life out of the drunks on their way home from the corner pub. He would be on the top of a wall in the dark, throwing stones, wailing like a ghost or whispering the names of those passing. Even the toughest men in the street would run like the wind fearing they were losing their minds or were having a ghostly experience. The next day they would speak about their spooky encounter with others insisting the alley was cursed with spirits of the dead. My brother listened and never said a word, it was his secret and brought him much joy that he had some power over these men. For those who were in the UDA, it was very amusing for us to see them dressed in their black balaclavas and khaki clothing with guns, practice marching up and down our street and looking mean. My brother would whisper about those he had scared the shit out of the previous night as we fell about laughing.

The dust that surrounded us as we disturbed the mountain of fallen pottery tickled our noses, made us sneeze and our hands and clothes were pure white. "Sis, get the big bell," my brother pointed with his elbow to where a dusty yellow bell lay. We gathered up as much as we could carry and off we went back to Florence Court, where we intended to sell our booty. We'd walk up and down the length of our street selling the ornaments from an old rusty pram that squeaked when we pushed it. The pram doubled as our go-cart or 'gig' as we called it and we had hours of fun riding in it.

Over at the sand pit the fun had begun. Wade's sand pit was just across the road from the old factory mill and it was used to store materials needed to make the pottery. It was a very dangerous place to be, but in our wild and weird world, it was the best fun ever. Huge steel beams supported a corrugated iron roof. The older boys would climb up the steel beams and hang ropes. They would then attach old car tyres to the ropes. We whooped and laughed as we swung from rope to rope and from tyre to tyre. Jumping from a great height onto the soft sand below was great fun. Eddie, the caretaker, used to chase after us, shouting that if we didn't leave, he would get the police. The older boys were always one step ahead of Eddie.

We watched in amazement as they dug deep holes in the sand, using any spades lying around and scooping it out with their bare hands. The holes were covered with thin sheets of paper and these were then lightly sprinkled over with sand. This had the effect of disguising the holes and it was only us kids who knew where they were. We continued playing, carefully avoiding the 'traps'. Poor old Eddie didn't have a clue that we'd be clever enough to set traps. When he returned as warned to chase us off, we simply walked out the back of the sand pit and watched as he fell down every hole one after the other, almost breaking his old bones. He limped about trying to get out again. We thought it served him right, but he was only trying to save us from possible death.

"Annie, Annie, come here love." It was Mehaw from number thirteen calling me from her wheelchair at the front door.

"Hello Mehaw, what is it?"

"Could you go to the shop for me love?"

I held my breath as I got nearer. Mehaw loved a drink and was another one who constantly pissed herself and blamed anyone or anything to hide her embarrassment.

"Uugh, what's that horrible smell Mehaw," I asked pretending to be innocent.

"Rex, Rex, get away you dirty dog," she yelled pounding the dog on his back with her fist.

"I'm gonna get rid of that dog, he's always doin that," she whispered.

"Did he wet himself again Mehaw?" I asked in mock horror.

"He does it all the time love, he's old."

I could smell the Tawny wine that Mehaw thought was hidden from my view. She kept it behind a piss stained cushion placed at her back. Mehaw had dark yellowish brown skin caused by sclerosis of the liver. She had shoulder length silver grey hair and no teeth. When she spoke, her top lip disappeared behind her gums and the wrinkles under her nose were pronounced as she sucked her lips in and out in a nervous breathless frenzy. Because of her skin colour and hair, we nicknamed her 'Tomahawk' as she reminded us of the old Apache Indians we saw in the black and white films we watched on Sundays.

"Get me one tomato, two beef sausages from Hoy's the butcher and two eggs."

"Can you remember that love or do you need me to write it down."

"No, it's alright Mehaw I'll remember."

"Make sure you don't forget anything love and there's a shillin in it for you."

I loved going to the shop for old Mehaw, well not actually going but coming back and getting that shiny shilling. The one good thing about Mehaw was that she always paid up. Some others would lead me to believe they would give me a shilling to run an errand and when I rushed back with their goods, they'd give me half a shilling. They were so cunning and they knew I wouldn't say anything. My mum would knock the stuffing out of us if we were cheeky to any of our neighbours. On the way back from doing Mehaw's shopping I came across old Dan Duppy.

He was standing half hidden in a dark shop doorway. The shop was closed and I wondered why Dan was there. He stepped forward as I passed and I could tell he was drunk. He was unshaven, he smelt of stale alcohol, his clothes were dirty where he'd fallen and his hair was greasy and covered his eyes. He peeked at me from under his filthy fringe. I tried to get some distance between us because the butterflies warned me. "Oh, hello Dan," I said, startled at his sudden movement. Dan had his hand down the front of his trousers and his zip was open. He stepped forward a bit more on unsteady feet. He looked left and right nervously, then back to me. "I'll give you this," he said, opening his hand to reveal a shiny half a crown, "if you give me a wank," he finished in a slur. I wasn't sure I'd heard Dan properly and I leaned in and cupped my ear for a repeat. He began rubbing between his legs and the butterflies told me to act.

I didn't know exactly what a wank was. I'd heard some big boys saying it and I thought it might be a bad or 'dirty' word. I thought that it might mean danger for an innocent child being said by an adult and the butterflies agreed. I pushed his hand away with "Fuck off Dan you're drunk. I'm gonna tell my uncle what you said you dirty old bastard." As I ran off I peered over my shoulder and saw Dan trying to escape on wooden legs that carried him two steps forward and three steps back. He resembled a living scarecrow except scarecrows don't get drunk and ask wee girls for wanks. I never did find the courage, or the words to tell anyone but I watched Dan closely after this and became very cautious when he was in my mother's company drinking at the local bar. Everyone thinking he was 'harmless' as I'd hear them describing him as such, including my mother. Harmless my fucking arse!

"Must put this in my purse", I thought, smiling at my earnings from running errands. When I looked at my money I felt happy. At an early age, I was hoarding my money, and always saving up for 'something'. I didn't realise until much later that I was effectively saving to help with my escape from Ireland and this early saving ethic was to stand me in good stead. Whilst my brothers spent their money from the pottery on sweets, I would stuff my pennies in a big purse. One I'd purchased from a 'jungle sale' of course. I thought that one day I'd be rich as my purse got heavier by the day. I had a special hiding place for my purse to keep it out of my mother's greedy hands. She knew about my purse and sometimes tried to manipulate me with her fake voice. "Oh, you must have plenty of money now wee hen," she smiled. "Tell mummy where you hide your purse, you know I wouldn't touch any of it don't you love." She was like the snake in The Jungle Book, without the lisp. She held my gaze as her wide eyes bored into me and began using her sickening voice trying to con me into giving into her. I didn't bother answering but I did run out of the house panicking that I might tell her because of the hypnotic eyes and the voice. When I reached the bottom of the street I shook off her hypnosis and cleared my head of that voice.

When I came home from school that day, I had the biggest surprise. When I opened the door, I didn't recognise my home for a moment. There were new curtains on the windows, a large brand-new side cabinet and a new sofa. "Oh, my God ma, where did you get these?" I gushed. I couldn't believe they were ours. We'd never had nice things like these before. I was so excited and started to collect the few clothes I had to place them neatly inside the cabinet. I kept opening and closing the cabinet doors viewing my items so neatly stacked. Yes, two vests, one pair of knickers and a jumper, all still there where I'd lovingly laid them. I was frightened to sit on the sofa but my mother patted the seat next to her and beckoned me. I sank into the cushions and giggled with delight. I asked my mother again where she had gotten such beautiful furniture.

When my mother began speaking I could tell she'd had a drink. She told me that we were starting afresh. She went on to say how she was 'definitely' going to stop drinking, 'this time,' leave Elvid and pay more attention to her children. Well, I just whooped in ecstasy. At last, my mother was seeing sense and speaking my language! The bad butterflies tapped me on my tummy and I shooed them away with a rub of my hand. They made me question why she'd had a drink if she was going to start afresh. I wrote this off as her celebrating our new goods and moving forward with a better life. If my mother says she is going to start behaving like a real mummy, why were the butterflies trying to warn me? I was a little anxious because I realised that the butterflies were not always bad and they seemed to try and help me sometimes. I ignored them because my need to realise my life long fantasy of normality was greater than the reality of my need to understand the butterflies' nudges.

My mother finally relented and advised me she'd managed to get the furniture on 'tick' or hire purchase. Perhaps the butterflies were aware this money would have to be paid back and they were worried my mother wouldn't be able to keep up with the payments. I had momentarily thought about this and I was mad at the butterflies for reinforcing my fears. Why were they feeding my doubts when I wanted to concentrate on the good? They tried to nudge me again when my mother said she had also borrowed money from the local loan shark, Isiah, or Ookim, as he was affectionately known to all. Ookim was supposedly a God-fearing man who never drank alcohol, never smoked and never cursed. Ookim was a scary old codger. He was about five feet tall and very thin. Ookim was always dressed in a long black or grey tweed coat. He had a deformed hand that he kept hidden under an old sock which he wore like a glove. However poor or cold we were, I would never have asked to borrow that sock for using as a glove in the snow. Ookim had a bald head and wide, bulbous staring eyes, peeking out from under his white whiskered eyebrows. When he spoke, his voice quivered and he had a pronounced lisp. He was a greedy man and when you had to beg from him, he'd make sure you paid what you borrowed twice over.

Mum constantly begged money from Ookim and when she sent one of us to get it, he'd stand staring at us in his hallway. Much the same way Dan had stared, except he was never drunk and there were never any requests for wanks. "Aha, mummy wanths money from Ithiah," he rasped. Ookim never let us see into his house and always made sure he pulled his living room door half way closed. I would strain my neck trying to get a peek at how he lived. I imagined his home to be dark, dank and filthy with the odd skeleton or dead body sitting on a sofa. All I could ever see was darkness and always, that funny smell. He took his gammy hand from his pocket and perched a small silver box on the back of it with his good hand. I watched curiously as he expertly opened the lid to pinch a small amount of pink powder between his finger and thumb. He had long dirty finger nails that snatched the box back into his pocket, having placed the powder on the back of his gloved hand. He brought the gammy hand under his pinched nose and sniffed hard until the powder disappeared up both nostrils, one at a time. It seemed that all the old people in our street used 'snuff'. I must confess that I had tried it once and it made me sneeze. I thought I saw Ookim's bulbous eyes doing a full circle. He shook his head as if to bring them back into focus.

"Ah, thath better."

"Want thom," he lisped, as I pushed his hands away carefully avoiding any contact with the gammy one.

"No I don't want it, it's disgusting," I replied.

"Five pounths, what does your ma want five pounths for?" he enquired teasingly. His eyebrows had formed two upside down V shapes.

"To get us some food."

"Hungry again?"

"We haven't eaten since lunch time."

"Let me sthee what I can do."

After some more unnecessary staring, out came the familiar wad of notes he kept in a back pocket.

"Tell her I want that back on Tuethday, pluth five more."

When we returned from school on Tuesday, the furnishings had disappeared, everything, gone! Through her drunken slurs, mum told me she had sold it all to pay back Ookim and to get some wine. We had to put an old torn sheet over the front window to stop the whole street from watching us. The house looked even more shameful than ever. The butterflies restrained themselves but did raise their heads as if to say, 'I told you so,' I could hardly bear it. With mum owing so much money, I had to work hard to hide my purse. I'll give you ten pounds next Tuesday when I collect my widows pension, if you let me have five pounds, she promised. The widow's pension was the one source of comfort to my mother after my father's death. I was tempted, I'd never had a whole ten pounds to myself before. I was so naïve and she was so convincing. God damn that woman and her manipulation skills. I eventually gave in and handed her the money. I wanted to be rich like Ookim.

"Oh, you good girl," she said dancing up and down.

"And you'll gimme ten back next Tuesday ma?"

"As sure as there's an I in the word goat," she laughed. I didn't know what that meant but I believed her.

"Ten pounds ma, right?"

"You know I won't let you down love, might even give you a bit extra for being such a kind girl."

She didn't spend it on food like she'd promised and went straight to the off licence. When the next Tuesday arrived, mum told me where to go, "you cheeky bitch," and I never saw my money again. I was bankrupt and heartbroken and I cried all day. Every time I looked at my flat purse and remembered how fat it had been a short time ago, I cried. I remembered lovingly throwing that purse up into the air and the glee of catching it and feeling that it was bursting at the seams. It would take me a long time to feed my purse to bursting point again, but I was determined that I would. I was hungry and with all the money gone there was only one thing for it . . . toast.

We survived a lot on bread. Toasted bread was warm and comforting and was done to perfection over the dying coals of our open fire. "You'll never die of starvation if you have the basics, bread, butter, milk and potatoes in the house," my aunt Winnie used to tell us. Well the good news was, we weren't likely to die, because that's all we ever had in our house. Winnie tried to find the positives in our sad little lives and she could convince you that you weren't really, poor, and that you just needed to be creative with what you had. In later life, I became more creative than Van Gogh.

Whilst mum was getting legless I sneaked out and went around to Mrs Dunn's house. She was a weird and eccentric old girl who loved a drink. She had short tousled brown hair and looked haggard with wide bulging frog like eyes, not a tooth in her head and she always had a fag hanging out of the corner of her mouth. When she laughed, her throat extended, her eyes looked like they were teetering on the edge of her sockets and she was all gums. She never seemed to smoke a cigarette, but like my mother and her cronies, when they were drunk, she let it burn down until she was balancing a long, fragile stick of grey ash. "Ah love I'm glad you called I've something for you," she said cheerily. First, she handed me a cigarette which I began puffing on, making circles with the smoke as I exhaled. I had come a long way from the days of stealing puffs from my mum's fags left unattended on the side of the cooker. I was quite professional at the old smoking now and didn't choke when I inhaled. I was on about two fags a day from the age of eight.

"Here you go love," she said handing me a doll. The doll had a straw body and a wooden painted face. She had black hair painted on the top of her head. I didn't like the look of the doll and thought it was old fashioned but Mrs Dunn insisted, "It's an antique love and will be worth a bit of money when you're older." I didn't really understand the meaning of antique. She was such a lovely old dear and I was too polite to refuse her doll. When I told my mum about the doll the next day, her bulging eyes, looked like they were teetering on their sockets, and she was very interested. "Antique eh? Take it down to Lillie and ask her how much it's worth." Lillie owned an antique shop just down the road. I was beginning to understand that antique had something to do with money. Lillie's shop was right on the corner near the launderette. I tried to peep through the window before entering, but it was crammed full of junk. The big wooden door creaked as I put my full weight on it to push it open. I found myself surrounded by dolls, teddies, jugs, teapots, vases, pictures, jewellery and other contraptions I'd never seen before and had no names to describe them. The shop made me feel claustrophobic. As my eyes darted all around taking in the vision of chaos, I noticed a sign that made me laugh.

> God helps those
> Who help themselves
> But God help the ones
> Who help themselves
> In this shop

"Hello ma love," said Lillie with a wide smile. Lillie was well known locally as someone with money. She had a doll like face that was well powdered and she wore bright red lipstick. Her hair was pure white and back combed into a high bouffant. Lillie staggered towards me trying to balance her bouffant and keep her composure. "I've got this doll who's gonna be a hundred years old soon Lillie," I said thrusting the doll into her hands. Lillie looked very interested. She felt for the chain that held her gold rimmed specs around her neck and popped them on the tip of her nose. She began scrutinising every inch of the dolls body, starting at the back of its neck. "Mm can't see anything here." Lillie slowly and carefully worked her way down the doll's body like a doctor.

When she reached the dolls feet she looked at my expectant face and handed the doll back to me. "Well, how much is she worth Lillie?" I asked, with bulging eyes and a hint of pure greed in my voice. Lillie laughed, "Bring her back in a few years when she turns one hundred and she'll be worth one hundred pounds, how's that?" I was disappointed that she hadn't offered me money immediately but amazed that a scruffy old thing like that, was worth one hundred pounds. My mum was eagerly waiting for me, "Well what did she say?" Mum was furious when I told her Lillie hadn't offered to buy the doll. "Oh, fuck it, I won't be havin a drink tonight then," she sighed.

I was intrigued by this doll. "Imagine, I'll be rich in a few years when she turns one hundred," I said out loud, rubbing my hands together. Although I didn't really like the doll I began to take good care of it. I made clothes for old wooden face and even washed them and hung them out on mum's washing line. I began taking her to bed with me. The doll's eyes were fixed and seemed to follow me everywhere which made me uncomfortable. I didn't want to hurt her feelings but I didn't have any real feelings for her, not the same feelings I had for my Tiny Tears. I couldn't wait for her to turn one hundred because I only wanted the money. "As soon as you turn one hundred your straw head is out of here and I'll be rich, rich, rich." I gently tucked her in beside me and carefully turned her ugly face to the wall. I couldn't resist a little trip down fantasy alley. I would be able to buy lovely dresses I yawned, smiling to myself as I knew there was a jumble sale coming soon.

I woke up hungry and helped my mother to build a fire in the grate. My mother studied me as I pushed a fork into the back of a slice of bread. I then stuck it to a piece of glowing coal. With a knife, blackened, from being used as the toast holder. I then smeared on some butter, carefully removing any bits that found their way on to the bread from the fire. "Stop that before you do yourself in," mum roared at me, as I smelled my hands. I had a slight addiction to the smell of the smoke from the coal. Mum told me plenty of times about the damage I could do to myself breathing in the fumes, but I didn't listen. The fumes were yellowish brown and I enjoyed inhaling their poison. On reflection, this act might be seen in the same light today as sniffing petrol or glue, except I don't remember getting high, so just poisoned then, not high. I was quite weird about smells and there were so many about, mostly related to poverty, alcohol, bonfires and petrol bombs. I had secret airs and graces although I probably didn't smell great myself and most of the time, the state of our home would make you want to wipe your feet on the way out. I wouldn't sit on the furniture in certain homes, I wouldn't go to the toilet in other's and I wouldn't eat or drink in some. I couldn't stand the smell of dirty people, breaths that smelled like shit or homes that smelled worse than dog kennels. Yet I loved smells like creosote, burning wood and Jeyes fluid. Jeyes was a very powerful disinfectant used to clean backyards and scare rats away, it was like fruity petrol.

Bonfire night and the UDA (Ulster Defence Association) were out in force. The UDA formed in 1971 taking up an armed campaign to defend loyalist areas from attack. "Left, right, left right, left right, left," shouted the Commander, as dozens of men marched up and down in unison. "Right turn, left turn, HALT!" Huddled together, they stood still, waiting to be inspected. They wore black, heavy boots, and balaclavas that exposed their shifty eyes through the narrow slits. Each carrying a gun in a black gloved hand. We nudged each other and tried to guess who might be behind each balaclava. These were the men that I call, the Mafia! Soldiers, fathers, protection racketeers, sons, husbands, brothers, arbitrators, criminals or 'hoods' and gamblers.

"That looks like Joe, no it's Kelly, no it's Pete."

"Shut up, do you want to get people into trouble," growled one of our neighbours as us watching children, tried to put names to the hooded figures. I was too young to understand their war and I couldn't take the marching men seriously. These 'soldiers' were just ordinary men without the scary balaclavas and when out of uniform. These men played with us, gave us money sometimes, kicked us up the arse if we needed it and protected us behind the barricades. Left, right, left right, left, right, left. These people were my neighbours, people that had families and children of their own, I'd seen them playing with their kids, kissing them, hugging their wives, playing football and rounders in the street, playfully hosing us down on hot sunny days, teaching us how to ride a bike, play fighting with one another, laughing and doing ordinary things, so how could they be soldiers, killers? No, I couldn't get my head around that. We took the hushed warnings seriously though and lowered our voices as we continued to play 'spot thy neighbour'.

However I viewed the Mafia, as neighbours and friends, someone was doing the killing. I'd witnessed the making of petrol bombs right on my street corner and even innocently tried to join in, offering to put the petrol in the milk bottles, as if it was a game, only to be pushed to the sides and told to 'go home, it's too dangerous for you' by those making and throwing them. I would watch from a safe distance as they pulled up crates of empty milk bottles, pour petrol inside, add a piece of rag, light it, then hurl it up in the night air, with great force. Men and women with white scarves around their mouth and nose hiding their identity. As the petrol bombs exploded, and through the flashes of fire, I momentarily caught glimpses of frenzied faces dripping with sweat. As a child, I couldn't comprehend that people were possibly being killed and maimed by those petrol bombs.

That night I tossed and turned in bed, unable to sleep because I was frightened. I could hear the commotion outside, right under my window. People running, screaming, bottles crashing, the sky was lit up with fire and the smell of paraffin threatened to choke me. My eyes were fixed on the window when suddenly, I heard the noise, click, click. In an instant my body froze and in slow motion, the window was engulfed in an orange blaze. My little brothers were lost in the orange. I tried to put my hand out, but I couldn't move. I tried to shout to them, but when I opened my mouth, orange fire came out. I floated down on the bed and I felt the cold blood circling my limp body. "Annnnnie." My mother's voice brought me back to reality. "Get up, you've pissed the bed." I rubbed my sleepy eyes awake and when I could focus, I was relieved to see my little brothers, fast asleep, the window intact and not a drop of blood in sight.

I'd heard about Catholics being tortured and killed. Felix Hughes, in his mid-thirties, kidnapped, tortured and shot to death. His body found in a drainage ditch in a place called Hoy's Meadow. This was an area where we played as children, walked dogs and fished. Hoy's was our local butcher's where I'd gone to get Mehaw's beef sausages. Eamon McMahon, a teenager, beaten to death and found floating down the River Bann. Again, an area where we played, right next to the beautifully kept Pleasure Gardens, where we went to play on the swings, 'higher mummy, higher'. Where there were colourful, fragrant flowers that we picked to make daisy chains. Sometimes bad things happen in good places. Those places forever tainted, robbing us of our childhood.

I'd heard about Protestants being killed. These were people I knew well, neighbours and those I'd grown up with. Sam Johnston, in his thirties, a man who came to my home on many occasions, who talked with us, played with us, ate with us, laughed with us, watched television with us. Shot to death and his lifeless body found in the Batchelors Walk. This was a magical, tree filled wood we enjoyed as children, climbing trees to snatch rosy red apples, watching tennis matches, secretly smoking and playing kiss chase. The first kiss for many of my friends was had in those woods. Sam was my brother's friend. When I heard my brother's sobs, I felt so sad for him. On the night Sam was murdered, we were all watching one of our favourite wildlife programmes. My mind was being therapeutically caressed by David Attenborough's raspy voice. I watched through my fingers, as a powerful lion, chased a cute little Zebra calf through the Serengeti. As the lion finally leapt forward and grabbed the calf by the throat, I began to panic. The bad butterflies clawed my insides. "Mum, did he get it, did he mum, did the Zebra get killed?" As was usual practice in my home and due to my sensitivity to death, my mother jumped up and told my brother to turn the channel. He did this as quick as a flash. My mother then smiled at me and said, "No love, they were just hugging." The butterflies told me she might be lying, but I needed to believe her. "Shush, shush," my mother's face drained, we had switched to the News channel. "Oh, my God" she wailed, "Oh my God, not Sam, not poor wee Sam Johnston." That's how we found out about his death. I wondered if the 'tit for tat' killers knew how much devastation they had caused, how much grief, how much pain. Sam was a somebody. Somebody's child, somebody's son, somebody's lover, somebody's friend, somebody's neighbour, somebody's rock. An image of Sam formed in my head. I saw him, lying there, all alone, frightened, confused, his body shaking, covered in blood, as his life slipped away, on that cold, wet, dark night with no-one to comfort him in his last moments.

James Liggett, an old man who lived a few doors from us, killed outside the Tavern Bar, in a drive-by shooting. The very bar my mother frequented, along with half the street. I had walked past that bar earlier and jumped, as I heard a sudden and very loud, jubilant roar, from inside. I thought maybe there was a football match on television and someone had scored. When I reached home, my mother told me through sobs, it was not a football match, they were roaring with joy because a young, Catholic man, had been killed that day. I realised that my mother had compassion, I also realised she was afraid to show this in the company of the Mafia.

I wondered, if my mother was afraid to show this compassion, how many others felt the same? The penny dropped, my mother was trying to teach me compassion, in secret! I felt so proud to know my mother didn't really hate Catholics. My mother, with her multi-coloured children of varying degrees of ethical legitimacy, her drinking habit, her foul mouth and bad temper, my mother, was human! I guess my mother had to make believe she sympathised with the Mafia, because this was her only way of 'fitting in'. Maybe this was her way of showing gratitude that they accepted her and tolerated her children. Although no words were exchanged, my mother looked at me as if she had heard me thinking that aloud. She looked at me, as if she was relieved, that I finally understood, the 'silent code'. My mother shook her head, "That was somebody's son, somebody's child." What a great moment, I hugged her tightly.

James Liggett's was the first dead body I'd ever seen as a child. I'd followed my mother to his wake and innocently walked into the room where his body lay. There were some people sitting around on wooden chairs. I couldn't see them properly because the room was dark and depressing. Out of respect, I fixed my face to reflect the gloomy atmosphere and lowered my head like I'd seen others do. I bumped into the coffin and everyone looked up at me. The bad butterflies froze me to the spot with numbness. I held my mouth to stop from screaming out loud. I was shocked at the sight of his long, black suited body, with white gloved hands, placed across his chest. He looked like he was sleeping and I wondered why he wouldn't just get up. People were crying, why wouldn't he just get up and they could stop crying. Heads bowed, the Lord is my Shepherd ...

That night, as usual, the Mafia were playing cards, in their office, at the bottom of my street. The office was a derelict house they had converted for their use. A 'two up, two down' catering for all the B's...the two rooms downstairs were for beatings and betting, and the two rooms upstairs for business and beer. They were fascinated by me and couldn't believe how well I could play. I'd learned from my brothers and was particularly good at poker. We sat in a very brightly lit room, around a huge wooden table. The men had ruddy red cheeks from drinking, they were laughing and joking around. I won a couple of games and think they let me win to humour me. When they wanted me to go home, I started crying. "Ok, you can stay, but we're playing big man's cards now and you'll lose all your money," they warned. I was so happy to be in the 'big game'. Sure enough, they had no mercy on me and in no time, I'd lost all my pennies from the big purse. These were grown men, I was a child, I reckoned they must be joking. I tried the puppy dog eyes, I tried begging and then shouting, but nothing would make them give me back my money. They laughed and ignored me. I ran to my house a few doors away, to find my mum sitting in her favourite spot, by the fire, on the hearth. "Maaaaaaaaaaa, they won't give me back my money," I wailed louder than a banshee.

After explaining what happened, my mum took me by my hand and walked me, in a fury, to the Mafia's office. Once inside, she raged, "Takin money from a poor wee innocent child, what kind of men are you?" The men held their hands up in mock surrender. They were laughing and trying to tell my mum of me. That I had insisted on playing, despite their warnings. Mum was having none of it and told them they'd better give me back my money, "or else." Some of them rolled their eyes in despair, but gave in, because they probably didn't want my mum to make a scene. They threw a handful of pennies on the table, and told me to fuck off. They made eye contact with me when they said fuck off, they didn't want my mother to think they were saying fuck off to her. Like me, they knew my mother's temper and she would likely have keeled that poker table over and threw their drinks in their faces. Killers my arse, how could I think of these men as killers? How many killers do you know, who humour little girls, play cards with them and give them back lost money when their ma tells them to? When we reached home, I realised why my mum had been so adamant in getting back my money. A bottle of the Tawny wine cost more than she had in her purse and she used my money to make up the difference. She promised the usual, "Don't worry love I'll give it back to you on Tuesday when I get my allowance." Mum was very happy that night and very drunk.

Geordie the yodeller appeared. He was as usual, carrying the customary effigy of William Lundy around the neighbourhood on his shoulders. Boom, boom, boom. Bands of Protestants were beating their drums everywhere and the noise was deafening. People were singing Protestant songs that told of their history. They sang about reclaiming their streets and culture and with every beat of a drum they showed how loyal they were to Ulster. There were hundreds of black booted feet, marching in unison, and men playing long silver flutes, to familiar lyrics.

> We are, we are, we are the Billy Boys
> We are, we are, we are the Billy Boys
> We're up to our necks in fenian blood
> Surrender or you'll die
> For we are the Billy the Billy Boys

Chris Dunn, the handsome leader of the True Blues band was as usual, expertly twisting his band leading stick around his fingers, behind his back, under his legs, around his neck and throwing it up in the air. The crowd gasped fearing he'd gone too far and would miss the stick on the way down from Mars. Chris looked to the crowd and with a teasing wink made his customary expert catch . . . and never out of. . . step.

The crowd erupted in claps and cheers. "Come on boys," shouted Chris, whipping the band up to a feverish pitch. They commanded everyone's attention and all eyes were on them. The competition for the best band was on! As other bands tried to outdo them, the noise became deafening. Hundreds of men, women and children lined the streets dancing, singing, laughing, some pretending to play air instruments. Whistling Jimmy, a loyal follower of the True Blues, was almost as loud as the flutes as he competed for attention. People were singing Protestant songs that told of their history. They sang about reclaiming their streets and culture and with every beat of a drum they showed how loyal they were to Ulster. There were hundreds of black booted feet marching in unison and men with pursed lips playing long silver flutes to all the old familiar tunes.

Billy Lundi was a very frightening character. We watched him being made. Every year, the men in the community would get together to help build this symbolic doll. First they laid out two long thin strips of thick timber roughly in the shape of a cross. These were nailed together before placing the donations of a white shirt and black suit on the wood. The suit was then stuffed with old newspapers, clothes and straw to fill out the arms, legs and body. Now Lundi was taking shape. An old football was used for the head. Long pieces of thin cream coloured rope were carefully attached to his head, resembling grey hair. A big black top hat was then added. White stuffed gloves were tied to the wood making hands and lastly his stuffed shoes were tied on. It could take weeks to finish and when the men were tired they rested the wooden corpse on an old gate at the back of our house in the rat-infested alley. Many

116

a time we caught a glimpse of the half-finished figure in the dark as we passed the alley on the way back from the shops. We squealed in terror at the sight of the praying priest. For this is what the doll resembled as he leaned up against the gate head tilted forward for support. When finally completed, Lundi was about six feet tall and weighed a ton. Only the strongest men in the street could carry him.

Lundy was to be burned for being a traitor back in the day and by the time Geordie and Lundy reached our street we had all gathered for the finale. Geordie mustered up his last ounce of strength for the long climb to the top of the bonfire. He looked like a Romany Gipsy with his dark olive skin, his jet black greasy hair and his crooked yodelling mouth. He was very strong and his muscles bulged as Lundy's weight bore down on him. His body glistened with sweat as he climbed up the bonfire. Clambering over old car tyres and huge planks of wood, Geordie finally reached the top where he hung Lundy up by the scruff of the neck. Windows were hastily covered with wet blankets to avoid being broken by the anticipated heat of the fire.

The smell of paraffin filled the air. The men in the crowd jostled each other as they fought to dip rolls of newspaper into the liquid. The crowd went silent as the men closed in. We heard the strike of a match and up it went. The sudden flash forced people to cover their faces. Children were pulled away roughly by their parents as the fire took hold.

"Burn the bastard."

"The fuckin traitor."

"Dirty fenian bastard."

"Burn him, burn him."

We covered our mouths as we watched the flames

reaching far into the night sky. The crowd roared as Lundy's feet caught fire. The roaring becoming louder as the flames rose up his body, engulfing his fenian head.

"No surrender."

"No surrender."

"No surrender to the I. R. A."

This was a traditional family affair and the whole neighbourhood was out. Tom, the street's story teller was there with 'Darkie' his faithful black Labrador and with his pipe firmly stuck to the corner of his mouth. I looked around and saw Amy Bell. Amy was a milder version of the witch in the Wizard of Oz. She was old and wrinkled and kept hundreds of black bin bags in her hallway filled with mysterious bundles of old newspapers and dog shit. I could understand the newspapers because many a time we wiped our arses on the News of the World, but the dog shit. . .. she didn't have a dog. Mehaw was there, in her wheelchair, with a blue striped blanket wrapped around her shoulders and of course her husband, always beside her, with his lips that reminded us of those stretched by wire and more commonly sported by the Zulu tribes we'd seen on television.

Over to my right were the Halford family and their children, all six of them. They looked scared and fragile, with dirty little faces and waif like bodies. They peered between their fingers at the sight of Lundy's arse alight. We often heard their screams as they were being beaten in the night, probably because they couldn't sleep and there was none of the lilac, coma inducing liquid available. Hearing their pleas for mercy, momentarily distracted us from our own pain, which was being inflicted, by our enraged mother and the dreaded belt. We weren't by any means in competition, but sometimes when one of us screamed out in agony, the neighbours' children would scream louder. The louder they screamed, the harder the lash, until all that could be heard were, stifled sobs.

Some people had put their furniture out in the street to ensure the adults had somewhere to sit. At some point in the evening all the children were lined up against a wall from oldest to youngest. This is the moment we were waiting for. With dirty outstretched hands and greedy intentions, we snatched at the crisps and bottles of pop provided by the Mafia. The adults were provided with bottles of the Tawny wine. The news on the street was that the wine had been stolen from a hijacked vehicle earlier in the day. Ah, this was the life. The barricades were up, so no traffic could come into our street. This allowed us to run up and down freely. The barricades consisted of metal sheets, wood and the occasional hijacked bus turned on its side.

Abuse or the threat of it, in all forms, was never far away. Tommy and Ben had lived on our street for years. I used to run errands for them and get paid with pennies for sweets or to add to my fat purse. One sunny afternoon a man called Peter appeared at their house. Word got around that he had come to stay there for a while. People were suspicious but were reassured by Ben he was, "alright." I'd been to the shop for Tommy and Ben and had come back short changed. I was good at counting but hadn't checked my change on this occasion. They had gone to the shop to investigate and had asked me to stay at their house until they returned with the correct change, promising me my usual pennies.

They were in such a hurry to get out and just left me standing there. The sitting room was very small just like mine, and I felt a bit awkward, because I didn't know Peter. He just sat there looking at me, not saying a word. I stood in silence listening to the tick, tock, tick, tock, of the mantle clock and stealing nervous glances in the direction of this stranger. The house was dark although the curtains were open allowing the sun to shine on Peter's face. It ran all the way down his long nose and made him squint. "Come and sit down love," Peter invited. "No, you're alright," I replied bashfully, "I'd rather stand." I continued to stand silently beside his chair playing with the light switch, pretending to flick the light switch on and off, to ease the silence and hide my embarrassment. Tommy and Ben seemed to be taking an awful long time to come back.

Peter turned to me after some more watching and asked again, for me to come and sit down with him. I nervously refused, sensing the firm tone of his voice. I quickly realised, he was not asking me a question now, and his voice impatiently, commanded me. Without words, he tapped his thighs and beckoned me with his hand, to sit on his lap. I didn't want to and my uneasiness was growing by the minute. "Come on love, don't be shy." Peter reached over and dragged me forcibly, by my wrist, on to his lap. He lifted my checked brown skirt up, just before I fell on top of him. My bottom felt warm and he started to bounce me on his knees. "I watch you every day, in your little dresses, walking up and down," he said, in a sickening and creepy voice. I felt that thing, between his legs bulging. I innocently wanted to engage him in a conversation about my nice dresses, but I knew he hadn't been watching me, behind those curtains, in a good way.

My mind flashed back to a jumble sale I had been to earlier in the week. "Granddad, can I have some pennies?"

"What for love?"

"I want to go to the jungle sale."

He laughed, "Here take this, for your. . . jungle sale."

I loved jumble sales and off I skipped to the old church hall around the corner. I bobbed in and out of the crowds going inside until I reached the dress stall. Ah the smell of mothballs. The wooden floors were unswept and there was a circle of floating dust clearly visible where the window let in the sun. There it was, laying crumpled amid some other tatt, the dress fit for a princess. I didn't mind that some old dear had probably died in it. I cared only that it was long and when I twirled around, it spun like a top. I couldn't wait to wear it. There I was, happy again, walking in my street, talking to myself and wearing my mother's stilettos, which were crippling me. I dreamed of being a princess with long golden hair.

The urgency and sharpness of Peter's voice brought me back to reality. The lump under my buttocks grew harder and Peter held me tightly, bouncing me faster. I could feel his repulsive, hot breath, on my neck. He began making weird, panting noises and rubbing his nose and mouth on my ear. "Go and close the front door in case any drunks wander in here," he said. He roughly pushed me off his lap and I fell forward, having to hold on to the wall to steady myself. I didn't know what to do or say, but I knew that I was in danger. The bad butterflies told me he wanted me to close the door, so no one could see, or hear, what he was doing to me. They were warning me to act! I had to get out, I had to escape from this monster.

I realised that if I closed the door, that monster would be able to do with me as he pleased. I thought I heard him unbuckle his belt. My mind raced and I was scared but the butterflies gave me an idea. There were two doors. The door in the sitting room, we called the middle door, lead to a tiny hallway before reaching the main front door, which lead on to the street. With shaking hands, I partially closed the middle door behind me, as I pretended I was doing as he asked. I then quietly, but quickly, got down on all fours, my knees weak and trembling with fear. The front door was ajar. I opened it just enough to squeeze through and gently shut it behind me as I began to crawl under the window.

I hoped that by now, Peter would think I was on my way back inside. I crawled along on my knees because I didn't want him to see me through the open curtains. He had already told me he watched me and there was a chance that he was peeping through the gap I'd seen in the curtains. As I passed underneath his window I was stricken with fear. My arms and legs were shaking violently and I felt sick. Had he seen me? Once I had passed under the window and crawled by a few other houses, I got up and ran as fast as I could. My head and my heart were pounding, I couldn't hear properly. I thought he was behind me, I heard someone running, I heard the footsteps getting louder, and expected his hand on my shoulder any moment. The butterflies told me they were my own footsteps and to keep running. I was breathless when I reached my house. I began to cry hysterically as I burst through the door. "What the hell," my mum began. I couldn't get the words out fast enough. "Mum, mum, Peter tried to touch me and he sat me on his lap and bounced me and I was frightened," I cried.

"Who is Peter?"

"That man who's living with Tommy and Ben."

"Why didn't you run to your grandda's across the way," my mum shouted.

"I was frightened of him seeing me crossing the road, cos the curtains were open," I sobbed.

"Did he touch you," mum demanded.

"No, he bounced me up and down on his knees and he lifted up my skirt."

"Dirty bastard," screamed mum.

"I'll show him."

Mum told us all to bolt the door from the inside and stay where we were. She then rushed out in the direction of my granddad's house. I was still trembling as I tiptoed to the window to peep out. After a short time, I saw my granddad, my uncles and my brothers marching with my mother to the house across the road. I continued peeping nervously and could see that other neighbours had been stirred by the commotion, some of them appeared to be entering that house too.

When my mother returned, she was shaking and very pale. She sat down beside me, then with tears in her eyes, she gently pulled me to her. She rocked me in her arms and stroked my hair over and over whispering, "innocent child." I wanted to ask what happened but the butterflies told me my mother was not in a good place and right now would not be the time. My mother stood up to light a cigarette. As she inhaled deeply, I watched the white puff of smoke, fly slowly upwards.

"Go out and play," she said gently and firmly, looking straight ahead and nodding towards the door.

"No mummy, I'm scared."

"There's nothing to be scared of love. No-one is going to hurt you, I promise."

I never saw Peter again and we never spoke about the incident again. I learned later that night, Tommy and Ben had been thrown out of the street also. I was sad, now I would have less pennies for sweets and the fat purse. I blamed myself and protested to my mum that they had never laid a finger on me. "They brought that pervert into the street," was her answer.

In the mid-seventies, Long Kesh Prison, later known as, The Maze, was used to detain prisoners of the Mafia on both sides of the divide. The prison was located between the counties of Antrim and Down in Lisburn. Prisoners were separated into groups, those who were incarcerated and referred to as, common criminals and those incarcerated for offences related to the troubles or the civil war. Prisoners deemed to be motivated by the politics in Ulster, were granted special category status. This enabled them to enjoy certain privileges. These privileges included being detained within their paramilitary factions, not wearing prison uniforms, not doing any prison work and enjoying extra visits and food parcels.

"Your brother's in the clink," my mum said, when I asked if she'd been crying. "Armed robbery," she sobbed into her hands. I found out later that day that my brother and two of his friends had tried to rob a local shop. I was angry and confused. I didn't want my brother to be in the clink. Mum received a visiting order and she was taking granddad and me to Long Kesh Prison to see Alan. My granddad looked very sad and frail, as if he had aged overnight. I overheard him asking my mum why she thought Alan would do such a thing. "He didn't even need the money Ivy. Sure, I would have given him money if he wanted it." My mother said she didn't have any answers for him and added that she was just as shocked. "My Alan plays football and he has everything," said my mother into thin air.

Mum was the first to be strip searched. Out came the socks from her bra and the prison wardens started laughing. "You can laugh all you want love, they're me diddies," mum joked. The socks were followed by her cigarettes and her purse. I was so embarrassed when I realised mum still had her nightdress on tucked into her trousers. The prison officers were in stitches. "I'm so skinny and there's not a pick on me bones," laughed mum. She went on to explain, "I need to keep meself warm." A female officer asked my mum if she had any money that would need to be locked in their safe, as money was not allowed to be taken inside the prison.

Mum laughed out loud and addressing everyone in the room shouted, "She thinks I've money. Do ya think I've done a fuckin robbery too love? No, no money and I don't even get me widow's pension till next Tuesday." She pulled her allowance book out of her bag and thrusting it towards the officer said, "Here love, put that in your safe and don't be runnin off with it." Everyone listening was choking with laughter and although I was embarrassed, I couldn't help laughing too. Granddad was being searched separately in the men's section.

We were ferried to the prison visiting rooms by bus. An officer showed us into a tiny room. It was cold in there and had long wooden benches to sit on. Moments later Alan appeared. He threw his arms around my granddad and they both started crying. Then he threw his arms around mum and me and then we were all crying. I'd never seen my granddad crying before and my heart was aching as he asked over and over again, "Why son, why?" I remember my brother was annoyed that I'd taken the day off school to visit him. I'd just started secondary school and he asked what class I was in. I said I was in class 1F and he was pleasantly surprised. 'Oh, you're not as daft as you look then,' he joked, tickling me playfully. He told me firmly that I must pay attention to my school work and although he loved me, he did not want me to come to the prison again if it meant missing class. I promised him I would not miss class again and that I would work really hard. He patted my head, 'Good girl.'

Chapter Six
Singing for Supper

It was a fresh summer evening and Tom was calling us. We all gathered around him. Tom had bronzed, wrinkled skin, and he sat on a chair smoking his pipe. Every now and then he would lean down to pat his dog, 'Darkie' who happened to be black. I was embarrassed when people called his dog, then burst out laughing, whilst pointing at me. I didn't like that Tom called his dog Darkie. Why couldn't he have called it Pat, or Rex or Rover? My friends and I, sat cross legged, on the cold pavement, our eyes bulging in anticipation of Tom's late night story. The street light flickered behind us, threatening to go out, but instead, sent dark shadows to dance around our heads. When Tom's story had finished, the finale to the evening included a walk under the old railway bridge, where hundreds of bats lived. "Right children, do up your anoraks tight," commanded Tom. I zipped my anorak up to the throat and tied the hood tightly on my head. I didn't want the bats to get my hair. The lice hadn't been able to carry me to the River Bann as my mum had warned, and the bats weren't gonna either! I was petrified of the dark and I could hardly see anything.

We all held hands and followed Tom's silhouette and voice under the bridge. Oh gosh, I wish I hadn't come now, I was so frightened and the noise of the bats moving disturbed me. "Don't let them grab your hair," wailed Tom, "or they'll drag you away." My heart was racing, "I want to go back," I yelled. "No turning back," said Tom, in a spooky voice. I had to go on, because if I tried to go back, I'd have been by myself in the pitch dark. I wasn't brave enough to face the bats on my own. I shut my eyes tightly and squeezed my hands in my pockets. It felt a bit like watching a horror movie through your fingers. The cave was alive with the sound of fluttering bats getting cosy and ready for sleep, or getting ready to tear us to shreds and suck out all our blood with their little pointed claws. It seemed ages before the fluttering stopped and I was relieved as we made our return and finally exited the tunnel.

"Well, did you go?" asked mum when I returned home. "Yes, I did, and the bats nearly got us, and I was so frightened and Tom wouldn't let me go back and . . ." Mum rolled her eyes in mock horror. "You must be really tired now love," she soothed. "Off to bed with you now." That night I slept like a greyhound after a race. Tom's ghost stories and the walk through the dreaded bat cave, wore me out every time. He told us stories of men who hanged themselves, usually in YOUR house, he'd point scarily. He told us of people who went mad, killed themselves then came back to earth as ghosts . . . and they hunt this very street. Tom would moan like a ghost himself and was always very animated. He told us so many terrifying stories that we were gibbering wrecks come bedtime, but we always went back for more.

When we came home from school, if mum was not at the house we knew where to find her. Mum would usually be in the local pub, barely able to hold up her head. The barmen had no mercy on us and sent us away if we came to get her. "Go on home your ma's busy, go on get out of here, no children allowed." We were desperate to see our mum and would wait until his back was turned before slipping in the door. Once inside, we could hardly breathe as the air was filled with thick cigarette smoke. The place was dark and seedy and the smell of tobacco and alcohol overpowering. That pub was the most depressing place I have ever been. You could almost touch the desperation, the poverty, the shame and the sadness. It was my idea of hell. I wondered why these people had been sent to hell, they must have done something very bad. Everyone was drunk and either singing or crying. She wasn't in the front lounge so we tried the back room. There she was as drunk as a skunk surrounded by her friends and singing.

When you lose the one you love
How lonely life can be
With such a memory ...

"Come and sing a song for Dan," she slurred, pointing at me.

"I don't wanna sing," I protested.

"Come on ma, let's go home we're hungry."

"Your ma's not goin anywhere," slurred Dan.

"Come and sing us a wee song."

My little brother Billy or Wee Bill as we nicknamed him, began to sing. It didn't matter what he sang because they were all so drunk they couldn't tell one word from another. Claps and cheers for Ivy's wee darkie. "Here you are son," said Dan as he pushed half a crown into Wee Bill's hand.

"Give that to mummy now and I'll look after it son," she

slurred extending a greedy hand. Wee Bill reluctantly dropped the money and we knew that was the last he'd seen of that. No chance of sharing a bag of chips now, I thought. "Ma, come on, please," I begged again. "Don't show me up now, be a good girl and sit down." I didn't want to sit in the devil's den. I just wanted my mother to sober up and take us home, make us warm and comfortable and give us something to eat.

Wee Bill continued to sing for mum's drunken cronies. I could never bring myself to sing for these people, like a begging puppet, for their entertainment. Even if I was starving, I would not sing for money, but my little brothers laughed it off and reminded me of the food it often bought us to ward off hunger. They sometimes earned enough to enable us to share a packet of crisps, or some chocolate or biscuits or fish and chips. After some more songs and no further offers of money we set off home. We knew that mum wouldn't come until she was ready. Once outside we had to navigate our way across the busy main road. The very road that had taken the life of my brother's little friend some years previously. Three little darkies, holding each other's hands tightly and trying not to get killed as the traffic whizzed past us, horns blowing as the traffic narrowly missed us several times. We had tried waiting outside for a while because we were scared of crossing that road, but when mum let us know she wasn't ready to leave, we were freezing and left. There was no use in us standing hungry in the cold, when we could go home and sit hungry in the cold.

Going home without our mother was not straight forward. Now we would have to face Elvid's evil dog,

Timmy, the Jack Russell, alone. Timmy hunted badgers for fun. Elvid fed him rabbit's hearts and let him drink tea out of the cups we used for drinking. Timmy was treated better than us and he even slept in my mum's bed. We peered through the dirty window, trying to work out what mood Timmy was in. As always, he looked angry and menacing. Probably because like us, he too had been left alone all day. I kid you not, we were ruled by that dog's moods. "You go first, no you, no you." When we dared to venture into our own home, Timmy would growl, show his teeth and circle us as if he was smelling prey. There were no 'dog whisperers' in those days. We sat as still as statues until either mum or Elvid showed up. "Ah what a great dog," Elvid would say, as he patted Timmy's head. The dog would wag his tail profusely and wiggle his body with excitement like he was having a fit. "He's a one-man dog," Elvid warned us. "Nobody else can handle him except me." The dog losing his mind to the sound of Elvid's voice and the touch of his hands.

Although that appeared to be true, on one occasion, Timmy was having an excitable fit that ended with him sinking his teeth into Elvid's ankle. I laughed as I watched him draw blood, as well as a fair amount of Elvid's flesh. "Good dog Timmy, good dog!" I laughed even harder the night we got Timmy so excited by a mouse, that he swallowed the thing whole. "Shake it Timmy, shake it," we teased. Timmy shook the living daylights out of the mouse and with us shouting and laughing it all got too much for him. He became manic, his eyes were rolling, he was panting and growling with fury and then in a flash, his throat bulged, as the mouse disappeared into his mouth. I was on my knees, praying Timmy would choke to death, and choking to death myself with laughter. We rolled around for ages afterwards watching Timmy continually retching as he tried in vain to regurgitate the mouse. Elvid had the disgusting habit of allowing Timmy to lick him right on his mouth, usually just after he'd finished licking his bollocks and arse. I secretly thought this might be a good time to encourage him.

There they were, the two lovebirds sitting in their usual spot by the fire on the hearth. Elvid and my mum kissed as if we weren't present. This made me uncomfortable and angry. The lovey dovey crap never lasted long though and when it all went horribly wrong we rejoiced! When mum and Elvid had a fall out, she liked to burn his clothes and I loved to help her. In my mind, if we burned all his clothes, he would be so angry, he would never get back with my mum and would be erased from our life forever.

Ah the heat, and the clothes were good quality too. "Oh, don't burn that love, that's his best one," mum would moan, as I sifted through all the good stuff. I would wave her away as I kept the home fires burning. That will teach him a lesson. Coming into come into our lives, taking over our home and beating my poor mum to a pulp! It wasn't long until mum was begging him to come back. She would pine away on the hearth for a few days before crying, "I can't live without him." I didn't understand why my mother needed him in her life. But looking back, my mother was a very beautiful woman. She was braver than most and fearless to a point. A beautiful woman, unmarried, with several children, of several ethnicities. Although I hated Elvid, I knew the other women in the street thought differently. I'd seen them flirting with him and laughing at all his jokes. My mother likely could not believe that he would want her, with all her baggage. I think that's why she put up with him, who else would she get if he left for good? Mum would usually then bribe us with money to accompany her on the journey to his flat to 'get him back'. I think I know what prisoners on death row might have felt on their way to the electric chair. You feel like you're on a regular walk, but you know it's not going to end well.

Mum didn't drink when Elvid wasn't around and she looked after us better, the way she had before she met him. When we saw Elvid after their splits, he too had not had a drink and appeared calm and collected, normal really. He tried very hard to win my affections. But nothing he ever said or did would win me over. I hated the way he brutalised my mother and I would never accept him or his brutish ways. I made it one of my life goals, to get him out of my home and by any means necessary! He plied me with money and cigarettes. Like other youngsters in my neighbourhood, I was on five a day by the age of eight and my mum secretly let me have them. She used cigarettes to bribe us. Mum didn't want my grandfather to know that Elvid was living with us. "He wouldn't approve," she told us. When granddad questioned us out of suspicion we repeated what mum told us, "He slept on the couch." We could tell granddad was not stupid and he didn't believe us. Elvid would swear me to secrecy and pass me a substantial amount of money. I would skip out of the house, head straight to my grandfather and tell all.

Elvid didn't show us affection, he certainly didn't love us, he didn't even like us. I could be in my house and not say a word to that beast for the whole day. As I grew older I had lots of words to say to him, but they were all bad. He made my skin crawl and I flinched as if he was an evil spirit, if he passed me. It was like having a stranger walking around your home, violating your privacy. I had no respect or sense of loyalty towards Elvid. It wasn't my fault if he couldn't quite believe it and that he kept the money coming … sucker! I argued with my brother's when I found them sitting next to him listening to his war stories. I was driven to anger when he made them laugh. I suspected he used this to get to me, as he could see the disapproving look on my face.

Elvid had just returned from the local pub and he was in his usual fowl and unpredictable mood. He eyed us with pure hatred. We were sitting together on the sofa watching television. When we heard the door open, we hoped it was our mother coming to comfort and feed us. There was no friendly greeting, no offer of any compassion for us hungry children, left unsupervised all day whilst he and my mother were out drinking. Elvid motioned towards us and the butterflies growled, even they hated him. His eyes were drunkenly sunk in his head and his lips dripped with spit. "Look at you, you're like a bunch of fuckin monkeys. If I was your father I'd …" Game on! I too, was fearless like my mother and there is no way on this earth he was getting away with that remark. I wished I could slap the last words out of his mouth only I was too little. "But you're not, our father," I rushed in, stopping him in mid-sentence. "You are just a drunken bastard who likes to beat women." He had a very deep voice that resembled the noise of the engine on an articulated lorry. Although, when he was sober, he could whisper like a woman. The familiar red vein threatened his forehead and his face became crimson. I could tell that Elvid wanted to kill me, but he knew I had two strong brothers and other relatives who were just waiting for any chance to batter the crap out of him. He had narrowly escaped possible death and the wrath of the street vigilantes previously. Having beaten my mum one evening and feeling smug with himself, he didn't know that I had bumped into the vigilantes on the corner and told them what he'd done to my mum.

"Elvid has given my ma a terrible hiding," I told big Hank. Hank was huge and the brother of one of my school friend's.

"Where is the bastard love?" he asked.

"He's still in the house."

"Go back to the house love and don't say anything to him. Do you understand?"

"Yes. Are you gonna kick the shit out of him?"

"Don't worry love we'll sort it out."

I went back to the house, safe in the knowledge that they were making their way. Elvid looked up at me as if he sensed I knew something. I sniggered behind my hand and tilted my head cockily to one side, looking him straight in his blood shot eyes. I couldn't wait to see the smile wiped off his evil face when he was confronted by big men! The vigilantes were always around but even as a small child, I was embarrassed to let them know what was going on behind our closed curtains.

Minutes later, three masked men appeared in our sitting room. I grabbed my little brothers and huddled with them in a corner. Elvid understood what was happening despite being in a drunken stupor and ran for his life, out into the yard. He attempted to scale the wall in his bare feet, but they held on to his trouser leg. "Come here, you fuckin bastard." He was beaten on his legs with a baseball bat before falling over the wall and breaking his arm. I was comforted by the fact that it was, his screams, I was hearing and, his bones, crunching, as they came apart instead of my mother's. He only survived because my mum became hysterical, pleading for them to stop and the vigilantes relented.

I had absolutely no sympathy for Elvid. I wondered what he must have felt, not being able to be in control for a change, not being the one dishing out the violence to a woman and having his arse battered. As he feared the consequences of beating me, he liked to torment me about my father. "Your dad was a jungle bunny who played a blow pipe to make music," he'd scoff. He would then blow into his cupped hands making a whistling sound and contorting his face until his eyes bulged. Elvid would then dance up and down the house, twisting and turning his body to imaginary music, making my mum and brothers laugh hysterically. He had a harmonica and sometimes he used this to maximise the joke. I was filled with rage and didn't find it funny that he mocked my father. I averted my eyes anywhere I could, to avoid watching him. It was torturous and I came to my daddy's defence. "My da was a boxer and if he was here, he'd knock your yellow teeth right out of your mouth," I spat. He knew he had my attention and now referred to my grandfather, who I adored, as 'that insignificant wee man'. I wasn't sure what insignificant meant, but I went berserk because I guessed it was something bad. I vowed to get revenge and the butterflies encouraged me that I should.

The smile was wiped off Elvid's face later that day as I tried to stop him beating my mum again. Elvid was no stranger to my temper. I jumped on his back and clawed at his face with my long, hard, finger nails. I pulled with all my might to try and get that beast off my mother. I didn't stop until I drew blood and quite a bit of flesh off his face. Whilst he was temporarily blinded by the blood, we made our escape to the bedroom. We were afraid he would come upstairs to get us and we hatched a plan. My brothers put bits of soap on the top of the stairs to trip him up, should he follow us. Sure enough, we heard his heavy steps. Intense fear gripped us as his huge, dark shadow, mounted the stairs. Around about the tenth step he went ass over tit, all the way to the bottom of the steep staircase. There was silence, and I thought he might be dead, well, I hoped really. Fingers crossed!

My mum slowly made her way down the stairs with us shaking behind her. There was blood on her lips where he had beaten her. His body was still and he seemed to be unconscious. We looked at each other with a mixture of fear and excitement. Oh my God, had we really killed him? Mum stood over him and quietly watched his body. We thought she was in shock at the thought he might be dead. Ever so slowly, mum bent down towards him then raised her hand in the air...bam! She hit him full in the head with her stiletto shoe. The brute was completely defenceless and couldn't move a muscle. Although we wanted him dead, we didn't want to go to jail. Mum laid into him and gave him at least one wallop for every scratch he'd left on her body.

She was going a bit mental and eventually we pulled her off. She was exhausted, we encouraged her to sit down on the bed and have a cigarette.

"Is Brenda coming out to play," I asked, when the door opened. Brenda's mum May, looked me up and down with her usual disapproval and closed the door in my face. Moments later Brenda appeared. We called for several other friends and headed for mum's favourite pub. We sometimes hung around outside the pub when we had nothing else to do. "No surrender," I shouted, impersonating the Reverend Ian Paisley, a renowned loyalist politician and Protestant religious leader. "We will not be defeated." My friends rolled around in stitches at me. "Do it again Annie," and I did, again and again and again. I had quite a knack for impersonating and I could take on the voice and mannerisms of most celebrities, including those on my street, with great accuracy. This was the face of the joker, the one that fitted in, the one I used to survive during my childhood. When I was being a joker, no-one was required to take me seriously and that's how they liked it. I was a somebody, when I was a joker and I got to poke fun at them, without being kicked to death.

"I'm sick of this pit, it's too small," said mum.

"Well you know what you need to do to get another house Ivy," replied Adel. "What about the house across the street, at number nine?" she enquired.

"It's been empty for a while now Adel, hasn't it?"

"Take the children down to your da's house Ivy and we'll sort it all out tonight."

"Have you got a sledgehammer then Adel?"

"Don't worry about that, we'll soon get one."

There was a lot of mumbling amongst the adults and several stood in the living room. I heard a great thud and almost immediately a cloud of white smoke followed. Everyone ran out laughing.

"Well we did a good job of that Ivy," said my uncle Billy.

"Stevenson will definitely not be able to deny you that house now eh?"

"Adel, come to the corner with me whilst I phone old Stevenson," instructed my mother.

"Wait a minute Ivy, just let me get me coat."

"Adel, hurry up or me wee children will have nowhere to stay tonight."

"Right Ivy, let's go."

When Mr Stevenson, the rent man, appeared on our doorstep later that day, there was a host of people waiting to validate mum's claims.

"Oh Mr Stevenson, the roof just came down, caved in. My wee son was in his pram and nearly got killed. Can you imagine that, a wee child killed in one of your houses that's fallin down around us? I did try to warn you a couple of weeks ago that this might happen Mr Stevenson. Don't you remember?" asked my mother with mock innocence.

"Dear Lord Mrs Yellowe, I can see what you mean. Fell down just like that?"

"Yes Mr Stevenson, just like that, without warning."

Number nine looked the same to me. I couldn't tell that it was bigger. The only difference to me was that the scullery was bigger and the tap worked. A neighbour gave me a single bed and some blankets. I was so excited because I'd never had a bed to myself before. In fact, I was so excited that I was ready for bed at six o'clock that night. "Surely you're not tired already love," said mum. "Oh, very tired ma," I said as I pretended to yawn. When I went upstairs I got into the bed and neatly folded down the blankets. I lay very still trying not to disturb my neatness. It was an amazing feeling, to be lying down in my own bed, with proper blankets. I happily drifted off to sleep. I awoke again, in the middle of the night, with a full bladder. I tried to get back to sleep again but my bladder wouldn't let me. I crossed my legs and squeezed tight, but no, I had to go to the toilet. I began to make my way downstairs, barefoot and scared. I hesitated outside mum's door. My mum had always warned us not to wake her up for the toilet. "You shouldn't drink so much before bed," she'd complain.

"Who's that out of bed?" she whispered. "Ma, I have to do a wee wee," I replied. "Don't go waking up the whole house, use the potty." "No way ma, I'm going to use the big toilet," I protested. The potty was my worst nightmare, everyone had them and I'd heard older folk calling them chamber pots. In my house, the potty was a bucket kept under the bed which was filled to the brim with piss, come morning. My mother didn't want me to wake up the other's and she wasn't pleased that I insisted on using the toilet. "You wait and see if the bogey man doesn't get you," she threatened. I was already half way down and nearly let it all out hearing my mum with her frightening talk about bogey men. I unlocked the kitchen door, sliding the small brass bar across. The door creaked open and in came the darkness. I ran as fast as I could having pulled my knickers down in the kitchen in readiness. The piss flew everywhere but I didn't give a shit, I was too scared. Tripping over my knickers, I flew back inside, pushed the bar across to lock the door and shot upstairs six at a time. I quickly checked under the bed to ensure the bogey man hadn't followed me and when I was sure he wasn't there, I snuggled into my new bed with the blankets up over my head.

1972 and everyone was in uproar over housing. The Protestant community claiming all the good properties were going to the Catholics and vice versa. Along with kerb painting, and sectarian murals painted on the sides of buildings, this was the beginning of a more visual segregation. Protestants and Catholics threw each other out of their communities, creating strongholds. The Mafia were actively supporting their community in taking property by way of squatting. There was talk about moving, "We're getting out of here," mum would say. There was a knock at the door, "Ivy, we have a house for you, get your things packed." It was Freddie, one of our neighbours. He told us he had arranged a lorry to transport us and our goods. We had to move fast in case another family claimed the house. I was sick with excitement. We were to be 'squatters'. Yes, we were moving out of Florence Court, or the 'Back Street Boulevard' as we called it. I had mixed feelings.

I reminisced about the wild fun we'd had, the bonfires, the stories, the go-carting, the snowball fighting, the cricket matches, the football matches, the hop scotch, the noise, the community….. the street. I looked out and realised, the houses were emptying of families and we were amongst the last left. The street was becoming quiet, leaving silhouettes where once familiar characters stood. I hadn't known anything other than this, Florence Court, with the back to back houses and the poverty. I'd sat in my home on many occasions, looking up to the ceiling, as if God was there and talking to him. I said, "God, you've put me in the wrong place, I don't want to live here, like this. But I know you're gonna fix it." Was this his work? Was this him, starting to fix it? I said the Lord's Prayer quietly, making sure I got the words right!

We were moving into a three-bedroom house on a new estate, in a place called Killicomaine. Elvid had a flat there and I'd been there on a few occasions to help my mother get him back, after one of their fights. Yes, us, the Yellas, moving into a proper house if you don't mind. We were excited as we packed our meagre belongings into bin bags and cardboard boxes. On a Sunday afternoon, we were carted off to our new house, tightly squeezed into the front of an old lorry, with not one seatbelt between us. My mother was a bit embarrassed that we had to move so quickly as it was Sunday. Sunday was sacred in Ireland. This was a day when no-one walked the streets, the shops were closed and no-one did any outside chores. Sunday was for church! Hanging out washing, mowing the lawn, cleaning windows ... all frowned upon, on Sundays. We tried to creep quietly up the path, as if we thought the neighbours might not notice us, with our blankets and trinkets, jangling loudly. My mother lead the way, walking with her back straight and nervously tossing her head occasionally. Freddie and the others trailed behind, laden down with other items. They laughed and jostled each other noisily, which made my mother shake her head and roll her eyes up to the sky. It was pitch dark inside as the electricity had been cut off when the house became unoccupied. Mum wouldn't let us walk around in the dark. We spent the first night on mattresses on the floor, with only the light from a fire in the grate, that my mother had managed to start. The shadows from the fire danced around the room and lulled us to sleep.

When we explored our new home the next day, we were overwhelmed. My jaws ached from smiling and I thought my mother had developed a tick, because every room we went into, she looked over her shoulder and winked, as if to say, how's this? For the first time in our young life, we had an indoor toilet. It was upstairs, right outside the bedrooms. So, no more pissing in potties or risking the backyard bogey men. We had three proper bedrooms and two gardens! A small garden at the front and a huge one at the back, very posh! We had an indoor coal shed and spaces inside and outside to hang washing. We had a kitchen with a big window overlooking the garden, and there was no more talk of the scullery! We looked out of what seemed to be a giant living room window. In Florence Court, we had tiny windows that hardly let the light in. Here, we had windows four times bigger. I had a little day dream and concluded, light brings light, and darkness brings darkness. I thought about this in terms of happiness. I felt happier in the light of my new home, having come out of the darkness of my old one. Being in the darkness made me an angry, miserable child, today, I was feeling different, optimistic. The butterflies agreed. We peeped out trying to get a look at our new neighbours. They knew who we were, 'squatters', 'them tramps from the backstreets'. I remembered the times we hesitated to go inside our home in Florence Court because of Timmy. Now we were hesitating to go outside.

The first time we ventured outside to play, the other

children gathered to watch us from a distance. My brother Gabriel, opened the front door and we followed behind him. They stared, they giggled, they wondered at the 'darkies' from the backstreets. They were frightened of us. They likely hadn't seen black people before and they wouldn't touch our hands for fear of the black coming off. I had first observed this fear as a very young child in Liverpool, when getting my Maltesers, and before I got lost. Some people, especially those who worked in shops, made us put our money on their counter and dropped any change in our hands without touching, or they would place the change back on the counter, to avoid contact. My neighbours in Florence Court, hadn't shown the same concern.

"Do you wash?"

"Can you understand us?"

"Do you have spears?"

"Do you come from the jungle or Africa?"

"Do you live in trees?"

Nothing much had changed, except we were now in a newly built primary school. The school was much nearer our home. On the first day, Gabriel and I had walked through the big iron gates. My mother had warned us to stay together. Gabriel was so excited and ended up letting go of my hand when he spied a friend in the distance. I lost sight of him in the hustle and bustle of the crowds entering the building. I was distraught being left alone and for a second, the fear of being lost in Liverpool resurfaced. When I finally stumbled into the classroom, Miss was not amused. During roll call the children were answering to their names. Miss called Edgar Bootle, present Miss, he answered in a high-pitched voice. Miss called June Todd, present Miss, she answered in a high-pitched voice. Everyone, including the boys answered in very high pitched voices. When it was my turn, Ann Yellow, present Miss, I answered in the voice of a tenor. All the children turned to look. I put my hand over my mouth. Where the fuck did that come from? It was like a scene from The Exorcist and I was the possessed child! That's the voice I had acquired through depression, aggression and being around my brothers. The kids budged up two feet, Miss looked at me for some time, under her eyes and then swiftly moved on.

Mum was drinking as much as ever and we soon got used to the shame of her being seen staggering around the neighbourhood by a different set of people. She didn't care whether we went to school or not. Mum was often too hung over to worry. I would play mum, and attempt to get the boys up and off to school. I didn't want them to stay at home because I knew she would stay in bed all day. I was smart enough to know that at school, they would at least be warm and have a hot meal.

"Ann, Ann Yellow? Get yourself out here," growled the headmaster, Mr Benson. He was a short slim man, with pure white hair on each side of his balding egg shaped head. His skin was wrinkled and yellow, like that of someone suffering from jaundice or sclerosis of the liver. He had icy cold, blue eyes and a pinched long thin nose. He dressed immaculately in three piece and usually grey suits and smelt of stale cologne. "Why are you wearing that awful checked skirt?" This was the same skirt I wore on the day Peter decided to accost me, it was my favourite. "My uniform is being washed sir," I lied. Granddad had slipped up and had trusted mum with money he gave her to purchase a new one. We'd thrown the old uniform in the bin. The money went on the Tawny wine. I threatened to tell my grandfather what she'd done. Mum swore to God I'd get a new uniform, next Tuesday, when she gets her widow's pension. She knew very well the trouble I'd get into if I went to school without my full uniform on. "Just tell Mr Benson that your ma said to go fuck himself," she'd roared with laughter, when I tried to remind her about the strict uniform policy. I was glad that Mr Benson had not seen me dragging my feet. Granddad had given mum money for well needed shoes for my brother Gibb and I. Mum had bought us cheap plastic shoes so she'd have money left over for wine. They didn't have our sizes but mum was not deterred, she just got the next size up. The shoes were hanging off our feet and we had to squeeze our toes together to keep them on.

In the big assembly hall, everyone stood in silence. They were right to be silent because Mr Benson was a very cruel person. He crept around the school, like a naughty child detector, with a long, thin wooden cane, tucked down the inside leg of his trousers. I was on the receiving end of that cane once. He lunged towards me and roughly grabbed me by my shoulders, shaking me, humiliating me in front of everyone. "Don't let me see you in that tomorrow," he roared." He looked me up and down in disgust and marched off down the corridor. I slumped into my seat, the tears burning my cheeks. How could he be such a bastard? If only he knew, how hard I tried to keep myself clean, to get to school, to do my homework alone and to try to mother three boys. Ann Yellow, I thought about this name, for that wasn't even my real name.

This name was forced on me by the school. My name being Annie Yellowe, with an 'e' on the end. I reckoned in later life that was pronounced by my African people as 'Yelloweh' to emphasise the 'e'. In their strange accent, Irish people pronounced our surname 'Yella' and we were known as the Yella's thereafter.

Old Benson had interrogated me one day for his own amusement, because he could. He was sat in a chair, arrogantly leaning back, watching me as if I was something to be studied. He began rolling his thumbs with clasped hands. "Annie sounds like a tomboy," he said, holding my fearful gaze. "And Yellowe, I mean where on earth did that come from?" Although that sounded like a question, his tone of voice warned me he didn't require an answer. After some more silent studying he piped up, "We will call you Ann Yellow. There now, that's more Protestant, isn't it?" So, from that day and for six long years, I was known as Ann Yellow. It was difficult to get used to my new name, but I had no choice. This was the first time I realised how much prejudice was eating away at my self-esteem. I was already confused about whether and how people loved me for me, and now my birth identity was being altered. I made a conscious decision that one day, things were going to change. I quietly spoke to God in my head and he said he was with me. The butterflies cried.

I was at the mirror again, with my school neck tie draped over my head, pretending I had long hair and dramatically flicking the ends. I squared up to my reflection and spoke to myself in what I thought was a London accent. "Elo, you awroit mate." I giggled, perhaps this was one accent that needed more practice. Studying my face from all angles, I pinched the bottom of my nose and startled myself because I looked like my mother. I thought maybe people would accept me more if I looked, more English, or more White. I felt a little deflated because I knew this was not possible. My friends had already tried to scrub me white in Florence Court and it didn't work. I really didn't understand why it wouldn't come off. When I was alone, I would turn my hands quickly back and forth. I was looking at the white side of my palms and then the black side of my hand. I was trying to make sense of what made me so different. I was tired, I wanted everyone to leave me alone and just see what I saw, Annie Yellowe.

"It's not your fault, that's the way you were born."

"You're not black, you're one of us."

"You're a nice chocolate colour, a chocolate drop."

"What's Annie?" they asked infants who could hardly talk.

"A darkie," the child would answer to a roar of laughter from all in the house. I had a pain in my stomach that wouldn't go away, it was called hurt, sometimes it was called hate.

Sticks and stones
Will break my bones
But names will never hurt me
When you're dead
And in your grave
You'll suffer what you called me

"Come on, I need you to help me get some things," said mum. She wanted me to help her do some food shopping in the town centre. Mum nudged me as a woman neared us in the street. My mother didn't like people staring at us and we were all quite sensitive in this regard. Too late, the woman appeared curious. As she was about to walk past mum started speaking to me in a language I didn't understand. "What, what did you say?" I asked puzzled. "Just say anything to me and pretend you are speaking a different language," she whispered. I tried to protest and thought my mum had gone mad. She nudged me in the ribs and urged, "Come on, let's have a laugh to see the look on her face." I began to speak gibberish, trying to fake an African accent. Mum replied, in similar gibberish only her accent was better than mine. The woman looked at us suspiciously and made sure there was plenty of space between us as she walked past. Mum was in stitches laughing. I could tell this was my mother's awkward way of letting others know we were her children. The woman was lucky my mother was sober, passing by us looking curious when my mother had been drinking, might have cost her an eye.

We had soon found our old neighbours from the backstreets who were also squatters on the estate. Some of them had become 'tenants' and their parents proudly showed off their new rent books. Our tenant's status was still a work in progress. My mother assured me it was just a matter of time and we were going nowhere despite not paying any rent. The plan being to withhold the rent until the rent book was in hand. There was some comfort in being around 'your own kind'. The local kids were discouraged from playing with us by their parents. It didn't last long though, because us backstreet children were fun to

149

be around and our charms couldn't be resisted. We were children who previously didn't have parks or gardens or toys. We were children who made 'gigs' out of old prams. We were children who dressed up in clothes from jumble sales turning ourselves into princesses and kings. We were children who 'fought to the death' just like we'd seen in the movies, with swords fashioned out of old pieces of wood. We were children who had fun in sand pits that became 'adventure playgrounds' that we made our own. We were children who had developed great imaginations to compensate for the many things we didn't have, things other children took for granted. We were streetwise children, resourceful children and yes, we were all, 'different'.

I woke up on Sunday morning thinking I might have wet the bed. "Ma come here quick," I shouted. My mother came running to see what the fuss was about. "Oh, that's ok love, you're a woman now," she smiled. Mum told me to get up and make my way to the shops for some sanitary towels. She didn't speak out loud, but like a scene from the two old ladies in a Les Dawson show, she mouthed the words, sanitary towels, as if they were secrets. Getting 'unmentionables' from our local shop was a very embarrassing event. I knew what to expect as I had been sent many times to get them for mum.

When I entered Jacob's shop, of course there were no females to serve me, "The ladies are on a break, what can I get you?" asked Jacob. He looked at me innocently with his gentle, red, chubby face and was so matter-of-fact in his approach. He always seemed out of breath and his thick, white eyebrows, set in such a way, he looked like he was asking a question. I glanced over my shoulder and looking back at him, I copied my mum and mouthed, "sanitary towels." Jacob looked a little insulted. Still standing at the counter, he faked a cough, and shouted out loudly, "Mrs Wand, six sanitary towels for Annie." I was mortified and slowly looked around to see the stricken faces behind me. Jacob pushed the pads across the counter, secretly wrapped in brown paper. The same kind of paper that was used for the butcher's sausages and for covering our school books. I was relieved to get out of the shop and away from the stares. Like a drug dealer, I squeezed my package inside my coat. A sharp pain shot across my stomach. I had a feeling the joy of my womanly discovery would soon wear off.

Aunt Winnie came to visit. She resembled my mother but she was smaller with a plump figure. She wore her dyed, dark brown hair, in a mass of waves, caressed into both sides of her face. Winnie was upbeat with an infectious laugh and a husky voice. "Oh, look at you lot in your lovely new house," she smiled. Winnie had orange lips, smelled of perfume and always wore the smartest clothes. "Has my wee Annie got her own room?" I took her by the hand to show her my room. It was almost my own room, except I had to share with Wee Bill, who was a bed wetter. It was so hard to stay angry with him when I woke up soaked to the skin. One glance at those innocent big brown eyes and I forgave him. He was still very young and I knew that my mum's lack of parenting had a lot to do with his problem. It probably didn't help when we scared the shit out of him as he tried to make his way upstairs to the toilet. "Look out for the man with the big green eyes," we'd shout after him. He'd run back downstairs again with the piss flying out of him and all over the stairs. We were so cruel and bent over double with laughter.

I was walking about our estate kicking stones and feeling bored when I heard Davina calling my name. I spun round and she shouted, "Wanna puppy?" I really did want a little dog and said yes. When we reached her house next to my primary school, four little black Labrador cross-breeds came at me. They were licking my legs and pawing playfully at me. One crawled right into my lap and I picked him up. The others seemed bigger and bossier than him. "Oh, he's lovely Davina. Can I have this one?" Davina said she was trying to get homes for all the puppies as soon as possible and I had better check with my mum. I'd been here before. I had a flash back to Liam, who had so cruelly drowned six little puppies in Florence Court. I shuddered, I was adamant, this little man wouldn't suffer the same fate, I had to save him. "Will you kill the ones who don't get homed?" I asked sadly. Davina looked at me in absolute horror. Picking up a pup to caress and kiss him, she turned to me and answered, "I would never hurt an animal. If they don't get homed, I'll keep them my bloody self." I was comforted by her words. My pup was tiny and I carried him back to my house in a coat pocket. To my delight, mum was thrilled and said I could have the pup. She gave me fair warning that he was my responsibility and that I'd have to walk and feed him. I called him Amigo, which is Spanish for 'my friend'.

Surprisingly, as vicious as Timmy was, he didn't bother Amigo, although he towered over his tiny little body for some time. Timmy sniffed Amigo's arse, "No!" "You dirty bastard, no!" Timmy gave me a warning growl but walked away. Years later, whilst watching Ceasar Milan, The Dog Whisperer, I realised they were just saying, hello. Amigo was a great joy to me and he grew fast. I liked to put him on his back on my lap, and gently rock him, the way I'd seen Elvid do with Timmy. Amigo loved this but I soon realised just how big he had become, when he started rolling off my legs. He was so big I just couldn't hold him on my lap properly anymore. I cuddled him to me and his furry body felt warm as he snuggled into my neck. Amigo was like a human being to me and it wasn't long before I couldn't think of life without him. He was a trooper and just as well. On more than one occasion, I'd left money with mum to buy him dog food and when I returned from school, my dog was looking sad and shivering. I found out that mum had spent the money on the Tawny wine and that my little Amigo hadn't eaten for the whole day. He was curled up on the cold concrete outside our house. When he saw me coming, he was up in a flash, running towards me with his tail wagging. Amigo was like a big horse as he jumped up on me and put his huge paws on my chest. "Ok, down boy, down," I said stroking him and trying not to fall over. When I realised my mum hadn't fed the poor dog, I immediately raided the food cupboard. In his bowl went eggs, bread, potatoes from yesterday and anything else that was edible. People told me that eggs were good for putting a shine on a dog's coat, Amigo's would sparkle after this feed.

I'd just started secondary school and I was pleasantly surprised and shocked to find myself in a middle of the road group. This group was made up of pupils with average learning ability and known as class F. I knew there were others who were brighter than me, but I had no idea many others were less clever. I watched other children I knew, being ushered into the lower groups. Some looked embarrassed, some bowed their heads and giggled into their hands, trying to hide their embarrassment. They called me to come and stand with my group, "Ann Yellow." I was not happy to hear that name and I remembered the promise I'd made to myself. This is a new school, I was determined to start the way I meant to go on, and things were going to change. I nervously knocked on the headmaster's door. I was ready for war, with my lips pursed in annoyance, my foot tapping and my arms crossed. When Mr Elliott bellowed for me to come in, I went to pieces. The palms of my hands were wet with sweat, my mouth was dry and I could feel the tears welling up. My legs buckled and the butterflies shouted ... act!

Even sitting down, I could tell that Mr Elliott was quite tall. He looked like he could handle himself. He wore what appeared to be the customary grey suit and shiny brown leather shoes. I sniffed the air, no aftershave. He also had the familiar greyish white bushy eyebrows, only worn by head teachers, mostly males, and his red face appeared to be indicating a mild heart problem. His huge office looked out onto the immaculately kept gardens that surrounded the school. "Welcome to your new school, what can I do for you?" he asked, in a firm but jolly voice. I was a little thrown off guard because I hadn't expected that. The words started spilling out of my mouth like Tourette's. "I want to be called Annie sir, that's my proper name and my surname has an "e" and I'd rather use my proper name if that's all right sir and ..." "Slow down Annie, slow down," he soothed. "If that's your proper name then use it."

My eyes widened as if I was questioning what he said in disbelief. Sir just gave me permission to use my own name! Yes! Yes! Yes! I leapt out of that office feeling POWERFUL! Well, I thought it was power, but it turns out what I was feeling was pride. What I was feeling was, ME! I strutted back to class like a peacock. I felt excited writing my name for the first time on one of my school books, and just a little bit naughty. I took my time when adding the missing letters and wrote it with a black ink fountain pen. I hadn't written my own name for about six years. The book was covered in brown paper from the local butcher's shop. The words stood out, Annie Yellowe! I smiled to myself. Now I had claimed back my own name, I was determined to do three other things, to get Elvid out of my home, to get out of poverty and to become successful in life.

The next morning I had a smile on my face getting ready for school. I looked in the mirror and said my name out loud, Annie Yellowe. I patted down my afro that was becoming a little out of control, and skipped downstairs. As I opened the front door, I tripped over a soldier with a rifle, lying on my doorstep, in the sniping position. "Sorry love," he said in an English accent. I nodded my forgiveness and straightened myself. This was a normal sight for us and the British army were here to protect both sides from one another. When I reached the corner of my street and I was sure the soldier couldn't see me, I started to tip-toe. I had developed this odd reaction on seeing guns. Soldiers walked slowly, with their guns pointing down towards the ground, and I feared they might accidentally shoot me in my feet.

"Oi you, you black bastard," Tyrone sneered at me, on

the way to lunch. My friends had told me to call on them if anyone bothered me. I went to find my backstreet friend Roda and told her what had happened. Roda was the girl who had tried to scrub me white, back in the day. "Where is he?" she asked. I led her to the canteen where the students sat at one end of the room eating, whilst the teachers sat at the other end. Roda calmly walked up to the boy and in front of everyone, she dragged him out of the queue and knocked him out cold. I couldn't believe my eyes. Not one person dared to move. The teachers sat in silence until Roda left the room. One of the teacher's picked Tyrone's limp body off the floor. Roda winked at me, ruffled my hair, cuddled me, then went off with her older friends as if nothing had happened.

I developed a sharp tongue and became verbally aggressive, a 'get them before they get you' attitude. I walked around with an aura of aggression that told people very clearly, not to mess with me. I called on my impersonation skills and used my wit to win people over. I became very popular with teachers and other students. Many of my old friends and neighbours I grew up with in Florence Court attended my school. Although some, never having seen a black person before, looked at me curiously, they generally didn't mess with me. Those that did, came to bear the consequences if my friends found out. They were fiercely protective of me. 'You're one of us'.

Despite my horrendous start in life, I did very well at school. School was the one place I felt relatively safe and 'normal'. I was voted for and awarded with 'prefect' and 'form captain' status. This meant my character was deemed good enough to run errands for teachers and to set an example to other students in terms of behaviour and achievement. I was very proud of these achievements and so were my family. At break time the boys ritualistically chased the girls. I didn't run very fast because I knew none of them were interested in me, the only black in the village. They usually went after Jules and Cindy, trying to get a grope of their diddies. The school was surrounded by beautiful Fir Trees and we used to hide behind these to smoke at break times. Diddies were groped behind the trees too along with stolen, awkward kisses. Our breaths stank of nicotine and our thumbs were yellow from smoking butts, or fag ends. When lunch time came, we would have to decide, fags or food? Often, we chose fags and survived on sweets until home time and tea.

Philip Dandy was in my class. He had also attended my primary school. He was tall and handsome with swarthy skin, dark brown eyes and jet black silky hair. His parents had inflicted a very unfortunate hair style on him and it looked like it had been cut using a bowl. I nicknamed him 'Bully Beef'. The name of a cartoon character in a comic book I frequently read. Philip had no time for me and however nice I tried to be he responded with, "fuck off you nigger, with your big lips, you fuckin golliwog." He always feigned an apology straight after and said he was joking. I was very hurt by those words and his behaviour, but I had a secret crush on him, and didn't want to have him hurt. However, there is no way on this earth, I would allow someone to get away with speaking those words to me. I had to put my crush aside and I began to stand up to him. The next time I observed him attempting to form the same abusive words, I quickly cut him off with, "look at your fuckin big lips, you nigger, you fuckin golliwog." Philip was shocked and embarrassed. He hadn't expected that. The tables had turned, now I was using his own words against him. The boys in my class roared with laughter. They pointed at him and ridiculed his arse. They laughed hysterically, shouting out that his skin was blacker than mine and his lips bigger. Before long, Philip was having a little taste of what it was like to be on the receiving end of abuse and bullying. Thereafter, when we fell out, he would quickly make up with me and beg me not to call him those names. Those names stuck, and the boys in my class tortured him. I added reverse psychology to my survival bag and the art of negatively emphasising 'difference' to defend myself.

I think Philip had anger issues because one day, whilst playing chase, he kicked me with force on my bottom. I let loose with a barrage of abuse. "Your ma's a drunk," he shouted. Others stopped to watch. I was shaken to the core, because no-one had ever said that out loud to me. The only people who knew about my mother's drinking habits were my backstreet friends. They never said hurtful words about my mother. Most of their parents either drank in secret or openly like my mother. This was school, my sanctuary, the place that made me feel normal away from our pathetic life. Philip had blown my cover and I was devastated. Now the whole world would know about my secret home life. I couldn't stop crying. In English class my teacher saw me crying and tried to comfort me. I told her what Philip had said. "She doesn't even drink," I lied. Miss said it didn't matter and no one would believe him anyway. I was so distraught and so was Philip. He thought I must be having a nervous breakdown with all my crying. He kept trying to comfort me and apologised. For once, he sounded genuine. The reality was, no-one even remembered the incident or what was said and no-one brought it up again.

I liked English class, but it hadn't always been the case. Whenever we had half term breaks, other children went away on trips or to visit family. We didn't go anywhere and this had been the case since Jimmy left. I would sit staring blankly at my work book. Everyone had their heads down and I was so jealous of those wiggling pens. Miss passed by, with her arms folded and smiling. On seeing the empty page, she said encouragingly, "come on Annie, just put down in writing where you went and who you were with to start." I laughed nervously. I was too embarrassed to admit, I hadn't left the street. I think Miss sensed my unease. Again, she tried to jolly me along. "Use your imagination Annie. Where would you have liked to go, the seaside perhaps?" Well, my imagination ran riot. I day dreamed a lot and if Miss was giving me permission to bring my fantasies to life, I was more than happy to oblige. Yes, indeed I would have liked to visit the seaside, and build sandcastles, and wear nice summer clothes, especially those blue sandals and eat ice-cream and swim. Before long, I was writing quite descriptive stories and despite my dysfunctional life, I was top of my class. Me, top of the class in English, imagine!

It was Thursday night, Didi and I were getting excited, because this was pay day for Elvid. He stumbled in, stinking drunk and we eagerly helped him upstairs. Didi removed his jacket and guided him to the side of the bed. She stood over him in such a way as to block me out of his sight. Didi kept talking to him, advising it would be a good idea for him to get some sleep as he had work tomorrow. He rocked forward, then from side to side and began fiddling with his shoes laces. His hands didn't work properly and were like closed fists. He wasn't going to make it. I asked Didi to help him take off his shoes. As the shoes came off, Didi passed his coat to me. Didi pulled the blankets over his fully clothed body and he fell asleep almost immediately. I was straight in his pockets searching for money. The next day, I watched him scratching his head and looking puzzled as he opened his wallet. He wouldn't remember what happened the night before and because of the tension between us, he would never think of questioning me. I would hear him asking my mother who he'd bought drinks for the night before. Elvid was well known for showing off his wages and flashing them around. He told my mother how he was never drinking again because he'd spent more than he meant to. I got the idea about taking Elvid's money after watching my friend Kelly in action.

During a sleep- over at her home her father rolled in drunk at about midnight. He didn't make it upstairs to bed and passed out on the sofa. Kelly and I had been in the kitchen making some hot chocolate. "Come on let's get some money to go dancing tomorrow night Annie." I was confused and didn't understand what she meant. It became clear as she tip-toed over to her father's side and knelt quietly down beside him. She tilted his body, just enough so she could get her hand in one of his pockets. I was shocked and angry, but too frightened to make a sound in case he woke up. It crossed my mind he might think I was helping her. With my eyes wide open, I signalled to her with a wagging finger to stop.

She mouthed to me to be quiet. Her father slowly blinked one eye open and murmured, "What are you doing?" My heart was beating like a drum. "Oh, I'm just trying to get your coat off da, to make you nice and comfortable," said Kelly, as she pretended to cover him up with his coat. Her father must have been very drunk because he immediately rolled over and went straight back to sleep with, "Good girl." Kelly winked at me and held up a ten-pound note. I waved my hands manically trying to make her stop, to no avail. Another tenner was held up and she kissed it before tucking it along with the first note into her jeans pocket.

On Friday's we had cookery lessons in school. It was embarrassing when I didn't have the money to buy ingredients. The teacher would make sure the class knew about my dilemma and make me wash dishes for others. The embarrassment was such, that some girls skipped school for the whole day or skipped class to avoid being humiliated. Elvid's reluctant donations on Thursday's helped and I hardly ever missed a class. We'd cook chocolate cakes, scones, bread and apple crumble pies. Didi and I loved to show off our cooking talents to two boys we had a crush on, Andrew and Sebastian who were in my class. Outside school they wore heavy, black, Doc Martin boots with rolled-up jeans or 'skinners'. On Friday, we'd fuss over them, giving them our pastries and we always bought them sweets from the funds we'd acquired from Elvid's pockets. The boys knew we were loaded on Friday's and we had their full attention all day long. They would never believe how Didi and I got that money and we never dared tell them.

Andrew lived in the same street as me and all the girls on our estate had a crush on him and his older brother. I was envied when my brother Gabriel became Andrew's best friend. Oh, the joy, he was at my house every day. Suddenly I had a lot of friends calling around my house to visit. The wind whistled as I closed the door in their faces. I wasn't leaving the house for a second until Andrew left. He used to sneak into our bedrooms in the wee small hours to play poker and smoke cigarettes. One night mum nearly caught us and we panicked and shoved Andrew into a wardrobe. Andrew had been smoking the very last end of a cigarette. When he eventually came out of the wardrobe the cigarette was gone. He was so scared that he'd put it into his mouth alight and swallowed it by accident. Andrew had blisters on his tongue, but we all had hysterics laughing about the incident and we talked about it for weeks. Andrew was one of the first boys I ever kissed. We used to play 'spin the bottle' in the big fields surrounding our local college.

Unfortunately, I had to kiss a few frogs before I got to Andrew. Six of us sat in a circle on the freshly cut grass. When we weren't playing spin the bottle, many a time we sat silently watching bees gathering pollen. It was lovely listening to their hum as they flitted in the sunshine from flower to flower. We also played 'rolly polly' where we rolled from the top to the bottom of a grass hill, making ourselves dizzy and falling about laughing. The bottle was spun and stopped at Ewan. He chose to kiss Kelly. She muttered under her breath and they disappeared behind a tree. The bottle spun and stopped at Andrew. The butterflies cheered, he chose me. We trotted off behind the same tree. Andrew gently pulled me close and we started to kiss. I felt his body shake with laughter. What was funny? "You're supposed to close your eyes," he said. He kissed me so tenderly, I had difficulty getting my eyes open again. I regained my sight and to my delight, he kissed me again. When we returned, everyone was fidgeting and rolling their eyes to heaven because we'd been away for ages.

Chapter Seven

We are the Tartan Girls

We are the tartan girls
We wear our hair in curls
We wear our skinners to our knees
We don't smoke or drink
So our mothers think
We are the Killicomaine tartan girls

"Wana be in our gang?" asked Roda.

"What gangs that then."

"The Killicomaine Tartan Gang."

"Who else is in it?"

"That's a secret. You'll find out if you join."

"What do I have to do then?"

"We have meetings."

"What for."

"That's a secret. You'll find out if you join."

"Do I have to do bad things?"

"That's a secret. You'll find out if you join."

"Is Dee in it."

"That's a secret. You'll find out if you join. Now stop askin questions, are you in or not?"

"Ok I'm in but if I don't like it I'm gonna leave."

"You have to get a tattoo first."

"A tattoo. My ma will kill me."

"Don't be stupid, you don't tell your ma."

In the early to mid-seventies disgruntled young people in my area began seeking recognition in groups. Some became members of the oddly named Tartan Gang, more affectionately known as KTR, the Killicomaine Tartan Gang. These gangs were springing up all over the place. Members wore clothes with tartan sewn on them. The tartan was sewn around the collars of their jackets and the bottoms of their jeans, worn above the ankle and referred to as skinners. They loved the pop group, The Bay City Rollers who also made tartan very popular. Some had their arms tattooed with the letters VT, meaning victory tartan or victory to the Tartan Gang.

I knew that if you joined a gang they might not let you out again, well not without giving you a good hiding or something. I laughed to myself safe in the knowledge that anyone who came across my mother would soon let me out when she showed them what she was capable of. My mother was very reckless and was well known for speaking her mind. She didn't care if you were the Pope of Rome or the Queen of England and you'd better watch out if she'd had a drink. Her tongue lashings were enough to send the hardest person into the nearest dark room to contemplate suicide. She would tell you in no uncertain terms about your ma or your da and anybody else in your family that she could think of.

"Andrew, I need a tattoo cos I'm in the Killicomaine Tartan Gang now."

"Shut up, you're not in a gang."

"Will you do it or not?"

"You have to put the letters V T on my arm.

"Ok, but don't tell your ma if I do it."

Later that day when my mum was having a drink in the

sitting room with Adel, Andrew came by. We sat in the hall on the stairs. Andrew had a little bottle of Indian ink and a needle. He asked me to pull up my sleeve and I did. "Are you sure about this Annie?" he asked. "Just do it before I change my mind. They said I can't be in the gang if I don't have it." He dipped the needle into the ink and was about to jab at my arm when I pulled it away. I suddenly had an attack of nerves. If my mum found out she would beat me. I pushed my head round the door. "Ma, I'm getting a tattoo." "Get out I'm busy," she replied. "Ma, I really am." "Shut that door. If I ever see you with a tattoo I'll fuckin kill you," she laughed. I was a bit confused because even though she had threatened to kill me, she was laughing. I thought that mean she was ok about it really. "Carry on then Andrew and don't hurt me."

I bit into my own hand to stifle my screams as the needle worked the blue ink into my skin. "Jesus Christ Andrew go easy, you're killing me." The red blood mixed with the blue ink made me feel sick. Andrew just kept rubbing the blood off with a tissue and continued with his work of art. "You do realise that you'll have this on your arm for the rest of your life," said Andrew with his brows raised. "Oh no, I'll get if off somehow if I don't like it," I replied. "Annie, you can't get it off," shouted Andrew a little too loudly. "Shut up or my ma will hear you," I whispered. Andrew reminded me that loads of other kids had similar tattoos and the girls especially had wanted to get them off. "Molly had one and went to the hospital to get it removed. They butchered her arm," said Andrew. Too late, the tattoo was finished and my arm was stinging like mad. It was swollen and painful to the touch. I quickly pulled down my sleeve and went upstairs to my bedroom. I sat there staring down at the blue bulbous mark on my arm. What had I done? I decided against the gang and regretted the tattoo immediately.

Didi and I got a part time job selling the local Mafia newsletter which encouraged the community to remain loyal. We didn't understand the content, but just wanted to get our commission. They were twelve pence a copy and we received two pence for every one sold. Many doors were closed in our faces. Mr Bradley always closed his door and would never buy the newsletter. On this occasion, he held the door open and told us our time would be better spent in church. Didi and I fell about laughing, linked arms and skipped on. Later that day, we were discussing how people did seem to be turning to God and the church. By the end of our talk, we were convinced our souls needed cleansing. Word reached us there was to be a special service in a local hall headed by the Reverend Ian Paisley. I had impersonated him many times quoting his famous words of, "No surrender. We will not be defeated." We couldn't believe that he was in front of us. Not being used to church settings, we became bored and started to mess around. When we were singing, we sang the loudest and made sure it was all out of tune.

Sing hosanna
Sing hosanna
Sing hosanna to the King of Kings.

We substituted with our own words.

No Surrender
No Surrender
No Surrender to the IRA.

Heads were beginning to raise and people were becoming aware of the heathens at the back of the room. When Paisley spoke, we sniggered into our hands and muttered loud enough for him to hear, "No surrender. We will never be defeated." He eventually realised where the commotion was coming from and promptly had us thrown out. Imagine our embarrassment, thrown out of church by Paisley.

> Amalam wooo black Betty
> Amalam wooo black Betty
> Amalam black Betty had a child
> Amalam the damn thing went wild

The words belted out of the DJ's box at our local disco in Thomas Street. I stood against the wall with my two girlfriends, trying to squeeze behind them to hide. I didn't like it when some of the boys teased me with their rendition … Amalam wooo black Annie, Amalam wooo black Annie … The boys were in the middle of the dance floor strumming their air guitars and nodding their heads. Those who could, shook their long greasy tresses about wildly. The room was in darkness except for the light that shone on the DJ. Where the light shone, you could see thick cigarette smoke swirling around and doing a dance of its own. We were admiring our matching red, white and blue jumpers that we'd had knitted especially. Suddenly the music changed and Bill Hailey teased,

> Come on let's twist again
> Like we did last summer
> Come on let's twist again
> Like we did last year …

We all had special jiving partners, mine was Val. Without a word, we extended our hands to each other and began jiving. There was a lot of competition on the dance floor and all the girls in there were jiving too. I was exhausted throwing Val all over the place and we were glad when Bill finished. As we left the disco to make our way home, we were becoming aware of a commotion ahead. Everyone was in good spirits, ribbing each other, laughing and joking. The crowd in front of us suddenly rushed forward shouting, "Get the fenian bastard." It was dark and cold and the rain was pouring down. I could make out the shape of a man who appeared to be drunk. He was staggering towards the Catholic side of town. I watched in horror as he disappeared into a sea of fists and feet. The screams were terrifying. I was shaking uncontrollably as I tried to pass the frenzied mob. The police eventually came and they ran off. I couldn't comprehend how human beings could be so savage.

The previous week, I had gone to a pub on the Catholic side of town. It was down a street we usually dared not walk as Protestants, but I needed to see Didi. Didi's mother was a Catholic who married a Protestant, so she could go into some Catholic areas in safety. "You can't go down there Annie." "Why not," I asked my brother Gabriel. "The fenians will kick your head in." I insisted I was going to make my way there. He shook his head warning, "you're just asking for trouble." I turned down Obin Street and a few passers-by nodded my presence to one another. When I reached the bar, I stood outside for a moment listening to the usual noises of people talking, shouting and laughing. I took a deep breath, then pushed the door open. A cloud of cigarette smoke temporarily blinded me as I entered. As I continued walking through the room, the noise stopped. I noticed there were mostly men there. All eyes were on me. Every head individually turning as I reached each table on my way to the games room. I knew my friends were playing darts in there. Why did the room have to be so far away and why did it seem to be getting further away the more I walked? Dark silhouettes sat surrounded by pints of Guinness.

Some had been playing cards and their hands were now suspended in mid-air. Some sat with their mouths open though no words escaped. I continued to squeeze past with, "sorry, excuse me please." The palms of my hands were soaking, but on I went. "Annie," they shouted. Didi spotted me and ran to greet me. I looked over my shoulder half expecting an angry crowd behind me. There was noise again. People went back to their Guinness, card games and chatter. I secretly breathed a sigh of relief because I couldn't believe that no-one stopped me, put me out or tried to kill me.

Puberty had hit and I was beginning to develop feelings for boys. I was becoming more aware of my appearance too. I started experimenting with make-up and clothes and I made huge efforts to look my best. Although a lot of males said they found me very attractive, few asked me to be their girlfriend. "Hey, big arse," Lavern's brother Jed shouted playfully to me. Jed was older than me and very handsome. I turned around to give him a mouthful of abuse. I thought it must be my pubescent hormones because he seemed to be looking at me seriously. "You know what Yella, when you grow up your gonna be a lovely woman." He added that I was beautiful and that other guys would be lucky to date me. He'd never passed any compliments before and I didn't know where to put myself. I ran upstairs to my bedroom and studied my reflection in the mirror.

I hadn't thought of myself as beautiful before. I touched my soft black skin. I ran my fingers over my soft black afro hair. I continued to my nose which looked perfect and fitting today. I thought I would look strange with a straight nose after all. I looked deep into my own dark brown eyes and told myself they were smouldering. I traced the outline of my well rounded and soft lips. "Yes," I thought, "he's right, I am beautiful." Some had told me that I was black and ugly, that I had big lips and hair like wire. Something changed in me that day and I began to think of myself more positively. Those earlier cruel words had been ingrained on my mind but I didn't have to believe them.

The boys who did show interest in me, I just didn't find attractive. I doubted that I would ever have a serious relationship. Back when I was younger and still living in Florence Court, Lavern told me she had feelings for my brother, Gabriel. She was confused about her feelings and said she would consider dating a black person. Lavern asked whether I would likely marry a white person when I grew up. I told her I wanted to marry a black man. Lavern laughed and said this would be impossible as there were no black people in Ireland apart from us. I told her one day I would find one, somehow.

We were in the lecture theatre and Mr Wilder was just popping out. "Just like your eyes," I laughed, behind my hand. Mr Wilder was our science teacher. He had an

English accent, a bald head and big bulging eyes. All hell let loose the minute his bald head disappeared out the door. The boys teased the girls, trying to touch their breasts and look up their skirts. My girlfriends, Cindy and Jules, joined me in the tiny bookstore where we began messing around. We were being silly, lying down on the shelves and pretending to go to sleep then we'd roll off and erupt in fits of laughter.

The noise outside stopped and there was silence. It didn't take long for us to realise that old Wilder had returned. We remained where we were, hoping he wouldn't notice we'd gone. "What a noise. I can't trust you lot to keep quiet for a minute and who's missing?" he yelled. We held our hands over our mouths to stop from giggling. We heard his footsteps, and then, his eyes appeared in the store room. Mr Wilder made a bee line for Cindy and Jules. He pulled them off the shelves, lifted their skirts, drew back his hand, and slapped their bottoms. I held on tightly to my dress and looked him full in his bug eyes. My mind flashed back to Peter and the butterflies encouraged me to stand firm. He got the message and left the room, telling us to get out.

I tried to show off my tattoo to my school friends on Monday morning. None of them were in the least impressed and some were shocked. Molly reiterated what Andrew had told me about her ordeal with tattoos. "Wait until you wanna get it off Annie and you will want to, believe me," she warned, pulling up her sleeve to show me the scar that was left when her tattoo had been removed in our local hospital. I was angry with myself and I walked around all day with my sleeves down in case any teachers saw my arm. P.E was the last class of the day. We had hockey with Ms Crobbet. I absolutely loved hockey, but my performance, Jeez!

"Annie, pivot, pivot," Ms Crobbet screamed across the hockey pitch, as I finally got hold of the ball. "Pivot, pivot," I mocked under my breath. There was no use in pivoting or anything else because as usual, the country girls were pivoting rings around us and were winning the game. We were pissed off! Those country girls could not be beaten. We mocked their accents, behind their backs obviously, they could handle themselves if they had to. We laughed at their attempts to be as cool as us townies. The laugh was on us because they cooked better than us, they ran faster than us, they played all sports better than us, they always seemed to have money for crisps at break time and they were so cheerful. Dorothy had come straight for me and tackled for the ball. I remember her big eyes serious and focussed. Her weather-beaten cheeks wobbled as she ran and her long thick brown hair was tied back in a ponytail. She flung out her stick and it caught my ankle knocking me to the ground. Ms Crobbet blew the whistle. "Stop play, girl down," she hollered, in her posh Irish accent. When she leaned over to help me up, her eyes went immediately to my new blue piece of flesh clearly visible as I was wearing my short sleeved yellow gym top. Her eyes widened. "See me after class."

"What on earth Annie."

"I'm sorry miss and so embarrassed."

"Why did you do it?"

"Dunno."

"What is it?"

"Dunno."

"Has your mother seen this?"

"No."

"You know I'm gonna have to tell her."

"Do you have to miss, she'll kill me."

"You should have darn well thought about that, before you ruined your arm."

As usual we shared soap and towels for the shower after hockey. Cindy let me have the last of her soap which was the size of a ten pence piece. The label hanging off the soap read, Imperial Leather and it smelt lovely. We all tried to hide our diddies and our adolescent pubic hair. Ms Crobbet cornered me as I tried to leave. I thought she'd forgotten about me. "Detention," she said, pointing me in the direction of her office.

Next day when mum was sober, she vaguely remembered me telling her about my tattoo.

"Oh, Jesus Christ."

"I thought you wouldn't mind ma."

"Of course I mind. If I'd have known, you were getting a ta-fuckin-too," she didn't finish that sentence, but continued looking at the blue mark, shaking her head.

"But I told you ma."

"What do you mean you told me?"

"When you were in the sitting room with Adel."

"I was drunk!"

"Yes, but I told you I was getting one, and you laughed."

"I probably laughed cos I thought you were joking."

"Well I'm sorry."

"You will be. Wait until the fenians see that, they'll kick the shit out of you."

"I'll hide it."

"How?"

"I'll wear long sleeves."

"You can't wear long sleeves when your swimming."

"You should have stopped me in the first place. If you weren't drunk it wouldn't have happened."

"Don't go blaming me. Get up those stairs and go to your bed!

We got news that a new teacher was to come to our school. With his tall, toned frame, his curly blonde hair, his dazzling eyes and his little gold earring, Mr Banks was gorgeous. He quickly became popular because of his beauty and the way he easily interacted with everyone. We secretly named him Banksy. Banksy was very skilled and made even the hardest task seem easy. He taught me patience and determination. Art became something all the girls looked forward to. "I'm really rubbish at art sir," I advised, when he was doing his classroom inspection. "Don't worry Annie I've got something to fix that." I wondered what he meant. How could you fix a crap artist? Banksy told me to bring in something from home that I'd like to draw. I returned the next day with an empty Kellogg's Frosties box. I wanted to draw the tiger. Banksy was very patient with me. He showed me how to divide my paper into four squares using a pencil. He then showed me how to draw parts of the tiger, one square at a time until the picture was complete. Finally, I erased the pencil lines and, hey presto, there was Tony the tiger drawn by me. It was unbelievable and the first thing I'd ever drawn that I was proud of. When I painted the picture, it looked even better and I couldn't believe it was my work.

Banksy said I should bring my finished painting to him,

at the end of the day. He was at the back of the store room. He looked up and smiled at me as I approached. He put out his hand to take my painting, and as he did so, he gently held my hand for a few seconds. My mind went into overdrive and straight to day dream alley. I was feeling strange and the butterflies somersaulted. "Fuck right off sir!" I thought I'd said that aloud but couldn't be sure. I threw the painting into his hands, and ran back to my chair. How could I handle him flirting with me? Was he flirting with me? Good old Banksy had got me thinking about sex.

I was dating Ronnie, who was older than me. Ronnie was from out of town and one of six brothers. He was small and stocky, with long brown wavy hair. Ronnie had lovely white teeth and brown smiling eyes that would melt Hitler. I first met him when I was young and he came visiting neighbours on my street. He used to chase me around with the other kids and kick my backside playfully. Back then, my butterflies tied my tongue in knots when I tried to speak with him and they made me giggle involuntarily. I ran into him again in a bar in Banbridge Town. He was a little more interested now I was wearing lipstick. On this occasion, the butterflies let the vodka do the talking and that had ended in a kiss. Ronnie had his head tilted to one side, trying to look sexily into my eyes. All I saw was vodka tinted red eye, mouth open … and … in for the kill. I'd been practising on the back of my hand, and I was getting good!

It all ended badly, when Ronnie decided to pay me a surprise visit, as I left school at the end of the day. Taking the short cut home with my friends, I noticed a beat up old red van at the bottom of the alley. Ronnie peeped his head out, beeped his horn loudly and shouted, "You look cute." My friends began to tease me and I felt embarrassed. They didn't know who he was. I'd kept him secret because of the age gap. I was mortified he'd seen me in my school uniform. I didn't want to look cute, I wanted to be a woman. I cut my eyes at him and signalled for him to go. He threw back his head laughing, before driving off.

School reports were due and I was excited because I'd worked hard. As expected, my results were great, A this and B that, well done, good results etc. I was sure I'd move up a class. I hadn't been informed of my move up to the next stream and I was sure this was just an oversight. I nervously knocked on Mr Elliott's door.

"Come in," he shouted.

"Hello sir. I've come about my results."

"All of the results are out Annie, didn't you get your record yet?"

"Oh, no sir you don't understand," I said as I pushed my record of achievements into his hand.

"Very good Annie, mmm, very good."

"Yes sir, thank you. It's just that no-one has told me when I'm moving up to the next grade."

"Who said you were moving up Annie?"

"But er, I just thought that I would be, given my excellent results sir."

"You've done very well Annie, but not quite enough to move up this year."

"But sir I've . . ." He cut me off gently.

"Your grades are great Annie and I know you'll get moved up next year." He steered me gently but firmly out of his office with a mumbled, "sorry, I have a meeting." I thought I must work harder. I was tearful and angry, but at least I'd still get to look at Andrew all day.

I loved the sound of the American accent, blasting out of an old tape recorder that taught us to type. Thirty girls in one room thumping out letters on the big steel key boards of our manual typewriters. Sir came around at the end, to check you had followed the recorded voice and all the letters had been correctly entered. "That was great," I said to Cindy, when the morning session had finished. "What's great about it, it's a load of shite Annie," she replied. "Look, mine's all over the place." Oh dear, Cindy's finished product was a bit of a mess. Sir told me how good I was at typing. He was so encouraging. "You'll do well at College Annie," he said proudly, patting me on the back. I was always top of my class in typing, even the country girls couldn't beat me at that! Sir had advised us that we would be doing, 'something special' for our typing exam.

I was given a sheet of paper that contained lots of letters and told, "Follow that Annie. Don't get confused. You'll will see what you've typed at the end." I did as sir said and followed the letters and his instructions. It took me a long time and several sheets of paper to complete. I was so shocked when I taped the sheets of paper together as sir had asked. The jumbled letters had turned into a picture of a huge horse with a jockey on his back. I was one of only a few pupils who had managed to finish the exam without assistance from sir and he proudly pinned my work on the classroom wall. My friends teased me with, "Teachers pet, goodie two shoes, geek." I didn't mind, my work was up on the wall. "Suck it up girls." My self-confidence was improving and I had nearly finished secondary school. I was top of my class in many subjects and I began to think about college. My teachers were very encouraging and kept telling me that I would do well. But secretly I was in turmoil. I needed money, new clothes and some independence.

I'd heard him crying in the night and had come downstairs to comfort him, as I often did. Amigo had a kennel in the garden that we'd lovingly built for him, but he didn't like sleeping outside. I would sneak down in the night to bring him inside and let him lie next to the coal shed on a blanket. Tonight, I'd put my hand down to stroke him when he was trying to eat his food. Amigo growled at me and I saw a look in his eyes that I'd never seen before. I was a little scared of him on this occasion. Elvid had explained he was eating and just trying to protect his food, like all dogs did. I eyed him with annoyance, I wasn't asking his opinion. The following evening Amigo wouldn't eat his food and I was worried. "Did you feed him ma?" I asked angrily. "Yes, I fed him and he was sick everywhere." I was worried about my dog being sick. "Looked like he'd eaten a chicken or something," mum laughed, "He's eating better than us," she roared. My Amigo looked sick and I didn't see him eating for the next three days.

On Thursday, Mr Elliott came to my classroom looking worried. "Annie, I'm afraid there's been an accident. Your mother has called to say you need to return home." My heart started beating fast and I broke out in a sweat. I thought maybe she had been drinking and had hurt herself. I ran all the way home and as I neared my door, my mum was coming towards me. She didn't look drunk but she'd been crying. "What's the matter ma?" She didn't answer but led me to the coal shed. To my horror my wee Amigo was curled up on some old coats next to the shed, looking scared and bloodied. He wagged his tail acknowledging me and although he tried to greet me, he couldn't stand up. I could see that his body was swollen. I noticed little wounds all over his body and asked my mum to explain. Through her sobs, she told me that he'd been shot by a local farmer. With a pack of vicious dogs, Amigo had attacked some lambing sheep on a nearby farm. He and the others had killed several of the pregnant sheep and their newly born lambs.

I couldn't believe that my sweet, innocent little angel was capable of biting let alone killing. I wanted to stroke Amigo, but I was frightened he might bite me. He was shivering and obviously in a lot of pain from the gunshot wounds. "Oh ma, what are we gonna do?" I cried. Mum told me that the farmer had warned her he would sue her for thousands of pounds, if we didn't have Amigo 'put to sleep'. Amigo had limped home and had crawled through a side window Elvid had broken earlier in the week. The police had followed him, and my mum had been forced to admit he was our dog. I heard a vehicle pulling up on the roadside. Mum shook her head and told me to go inside. "What's happening ma?" I asked suspiciously. Two men appeared at the door with a long wooden stick, bearing a hoop at the end. The hoop was around Amigo's neck in seconds and he was hauled to his feet. "Don't do that," I screamed, "You're hurting him." One of the men calmly told me that he would be, "put out of his misery humanely." "What does he mean ma?" My mum explained that she didn't have any money to give to the farmer as compensation and the only way to avoid any further action, was to have Amigo killed.

I was devastated watching him disappear, in agony with two strangers partly strangling him. I felt sorry for the poor sheep, but I was sorry for my dog too. My mum was crying and so was I. Amigo watched us all the way down the path, as he limped to his death. His little eyes had a look of fear like he was begging us to save him. The van drove off and my mum almost fainted. I hadn't realised that my mother cared so much for Amigo. We thought about the night he was sick. That must have been the remains of the sheep he was vomiting up. We had a cup of tea together and tried to go over the events leading up to Amigo's death. The police later told us, once a dog gets the taste of blood, they become killers and can't stop. So, it seemed there was no other option and that my wee Amigo had to die. Rest in peace my little man.

I spent the next year at Lurgan Road Technical College. It was very different from my secondary school. I found the time-table confusing and half the time I had no idea what class I was supposed to be in. The building was massive, there were so many students and I didn't bond with any of the teachers. I felt lost and deflated. I couldn't cope with the independence required to be at college. Apart from flirting with the older boys from the Training Centre next door, I had lost interest in any further education. For the first time in my school life, I started bunking off. Word reached the headmaster that Annie Yellowe was previously a very good and able student who appeared to lack enthusiasm. I was summoned to speak with him.

I told the headmaster, "I have decided to leave college as

soon as possible and I'm looking for work." Mr Tott was very disappointed in me, but my mind was made up. "You're going to regret this Annie," cautioned Mr Tott. I stood there stiff, adamant that whatever he said would make no difference. Mr Tott reluctantly added my name to the 'pre-employment' list. This was a programme that enabled students to go out into the community to gain unpaid work experience. I was tired of living in a shabby house. I was tired of worrying myself sick over unpaid bills. I was tired of being cold and miserable. I was scared that because I was black, I would never be considered for work in Northern Ireland. What would I do then?

The Ulster Carpet Mills was a local factory based in Garvaghy Road, and one of the major employers in my town. They produced woollen Axminster carpets and to my delight they selected me from the college programme. Just before I turned sixteen, I received news that they were offering me full time employment, to start immediately. I felt proud as I looked at myself in my new factory outfit. 'The Ulster Carpet Mills' logo, was proudly displayed on the front of the dark blue pinafore. I was excited at the prospect of earning my own money. A lot of the girls from my estate worked there and I was comforted by this. The machinery looked big and daunting, but before long I had been shown how to operate the 'loom'. The loom had long tubular lights that ran under a clear Perspex cover for about two metres. The lights blinded me and the heat from them was unbearable. Above the lights were several metal spikes that held the colourful threaded bobbins used to repair any faults in the carpet.

It was my job as a 'Darner' to fix any holes in the carpets, that showed up under the lights. We had to stand all day in a box that was just big enough to turn around in and this put a huge strain on my legs. When the pain became too much and my legs ached from walking up and down the tiny isle, I would join the others for a break. The smoking room was a small steel cage on the ground floor. It was ventilated by four large open panels that provided a view of hundreds of colourful carpets, rolled up and occupying the floor space and under the isles. The place reeked of stale smoke, and cigarette ends covered the dirty floor. Waldo, the floor supervisor, claimed his regular spot in the corner and stood smoking his pipe, in deep thought. This little steel cage is where the men and women came together, to socialise, to have a fag and a break from the heat of the lights and the pain of carpet burns. Some were flirting, some were play fighting, some gossiping and some just silently staring into space. Catholics and Protestants working together, everyone trying to earn a living to support their families. We could work side by side, socialise in the factory bar side by side, but we couldn't live side by side. I was becoming restless and I looked forward to the end of every day. There was no enjoyment for me, other than the pay check at the end of the week and going out dancing.

We had a great time getting ready to go out. Top of the Pops was on the telly and all our friends had gathered in my house, as was the norm. Our house was an open one, and was usually bursting at the seams with other kids. We had put our money together to get alcohol to help with the old 'Dutch courage'. There was Vodka, my friend Fran's favourite, cider, Wee Bill's favourite, and lager, everyone's favourite when all else had gone. As I put the finishing touches to my lipstick and patted my afro down a little, the Jackson's came on. I turned the music up full blast and did a 360-degree pivot on one foot, that even Ms Crobbet would have been proud of. My brothers began showing off some cool moves to our friends. My mother looked on with admiration, laughing and clapping her hands in between sips of Vodka. Wee Bill moon walked, Gabriel body popped and Wilson disco danced. We were in stitches as it became a free-for-all, with each one trying to outdo the other. Fran reminded us about the time and we left together to make the last bus to Banbridge Town where the nightclub was. The bus was packed with locals and we knew most of the people on there. Most were drinking beer and wine openly from bottles and cans. The banter on the way was great as we called out teasing each other mercilessly. "Next stop," we shouted in unison, to the bus driver, and he pulled into the kerb.

We regularly had to hitch a lift home as we seldom could afford a cab. Everton, a guy I knew quite well, approached me at the end of the dance and offered to take me home in his car. Of course, I was delighted and accepted. I didn't remember seeing Fran and assumed she would get home with my brothers and our other friends. He opened the car door and I drunkenly slumped into the passenger side. On the way back home, Everton had turned the heat up so much that I was gasping for air. He pulled over into a dark cul-de-sac saying he was going to help me take off my jacket. As he slid my coat off, he started to kiss me. It was unexpected, but I responded. Everton must have taken this as a sign to go further and he began to unbutton my top. I tried to protest, but he told me not to worry, everything would be alright.

Chapter Eight

Bad News at the Surgery

Now that I was earning my own money, I'd been able to afford a few holidays to Spain. We stayed in basic, low budget apartments for two alcohol fuelled weeks. I longed for something better and classier. I worked overtime from six in the morning to nine at night, trying to earn enough money to fix up our house. My brothers said they would help to do the decorating and contribute to the purchasing of the materials. They didn't help though and I was forced to manage everything alone. I began to feel used by my family. I resented the fact that I was the only one bringing in money and they were benefiting from my hard work. As I had no-one to help, I'd hold the wallpaper on my head and push it up the wall as best as I could. I was exhausted having worked all day at the factory, but determined to make our home beautiful. I don't know how, because I had never decorated in my life, but I managed to complete the whole house alone. To my amazement, the wallpaper stayed on, the paint didn't run and when I'd finished, I stepped back and admired my work with pride. I bought new carpets, new furniture and I got us a phone. Before long, our home was transformed.

I missed a period and I was absolutely petrified. Ever since the night with Everton, I had prayed to God, "please don't let me be pregnant. I will never do such a thing again." I didn't tell a soul, I was too scared and ashamed. I made an appointment to see my doctor. When I reached his surgery, Alison was on reception. I was nervous because I knew her well from my school. "Hi Annie what can we do for you?" I told her that I had an appointment. "What's it for?" she asked. Don't worry what it's for you nosey bitch, I thought. "It's private," I stuttered. Alison was not pleased about me refusing to share my reasons for seeing the doctor with her. She pointed me to the waiting area. I sat there looking down at the floor wishing it was all a bad dream. "Annie Yellowe," shouted the doctor. I looked around anxiously. I was annoyed he had shouted my name so loudly, there might be someone in the surgery who knew me.

I had to leave his room to do a pregnancy test requiring me to urinate in a tube. I hurried past reception and into the toilet. I was paranoid and glanced over at Alison. I thought she might guess why I was going in there. I slid the tube up the inside of my sleeve. Doctor said I'd done a good job and the results would be back next week. I wasn't pleased that I had to wait, but doctor said it couldn't be done any quicker. Doctor was sympathetic when I told him that I knew Alison and she would read my name on the tube and might tell someone. "Alison is bound by confidential rules here," he offered, trying to appease me. I started to cry and doctor had a solution. "Put a different name on the tube and instead of coming back in to the surgery, phone in, for your results." I was satisfied this might work. Tina Potter, I wrote on the tube. "Don't forget the name you'll be using," whispered doctor as he walked me to the exit.

I sat on the side of my bed twisting and wringing my

hands. I was frightened to pick up the phone because I
didn't know if Alison was on reception today. I knew I had
to get on with it. I put some cotton wool inside my mouth
to try and disguise my voice should Alison pick up the
phone. I nervously dialled the number and in a shaky voice
I said, "Oh hello. I'm calling to get the results of a
pregnancy test." Alison answered, she didn't say her name
but I knew it was her. "What name please?" My stomach
was churning and I thought she had worked out who I was.
It also crossed my mind that doctor might have told her
behind my back. "Tina Potter," I said in a low voice. "Bear
with me." I heard some ruffling and moments later, "You'll
be delighted to know that the test was positive and you are
pregnant," said Alison.

My body went cold as I replaced the receiver in its cradle.
I removed the cotton wool and put my head in my hands in
floods of tears. I was crying as quietly as I could because my
mum was downstairs and she might hear me. I thought
about telling her, but quickly dismissed the idea. Mum was
not good at keeping secrets and I feared she might ridicule
me and tell everyone. I thought others might judge me for
having a child out of wedlock, the way some had judged my
mother back in the past and many others since that time.

I went over things again and again in my mind. I didn't
want to have a baby for someone I didn't love, I didn't feel
capable of looking after a child and I didn't want to tell
Everton. I wouldn't bother anyone, I wouldn't tell anyone
and it would all go away if I simply told myself it wasn't
true. I knew the consequences of this, I'd seen it in a
documentary. I started to think about abortion. This was a
situation I never believed I would ever have to contemplate.

I thought about the documentary and I knew I had to act fast. I realised that I couldn't do this alone. Finally, I decided to confide in my aunt Winnie. Hadn't she always been good to me? She had rescued me from the scenes of drunken brawls between Elvid and my mum many times. Winnie would take me to her little cottage out in the countryside and keep me there for the whole weekend. I enjoyed my time at my aunt Winnie's. I slept beside her and she told me stories about her own children and how they'd grown up. She let me see and play with some of their old toys that lived in the attic and she fed me well.

I phoned Winnie and said I had something important to discuss with her. Aunt Winnie came to see me on the Saturday night. My mum was suspicious when we went out for a walk but she didn't question me. Winnie was more shocked that I'd had sex than the fact I was pregnant. She told me not to cry and that she would make everything go away quickly. "Don't you worry love, I'll sort it out," she soothed. I needed to hear those words and I clung to them. Winnie promised me she wouldn't tell my mother or anybody she didn't need to. Uncle Herbie, her husband, would have to know though, he'd be taking us somewhere to 'sort it'. I was ashamed my uncle would know that I'd had sex and feared he wouldn't help me. We didn't say a word in the car until we reached a huge period house much like the cruelty man's. The pebbles crunched under the wheels of our car as we pulled in. Winnie told me this was the home of a well-known doctor many had used over the years. "Will he be able to take the baby away?" I asked. Winnie assured me that when doctor had finished with me I'd be fine.

I was ushered into a darkened room and doctor asked Winnie to leave. I felt awkward and embarrassed because I didn't know him. He donned rubber gloves and asked me to get up on the table. Once I'd done as he asked he produced a long steel rod and began to insert it slowly. I flinched with the pain but he assured me all would be fine. After what seemed like an age doctor told me to get dressed. He removed his gloves and carefully washed his hands. When aunt Winnie entered the room again doctor shook his head slowly and said my womb was 'slanting' and that he wouldn't be able to perform a satisfactory termination for fear of damaging me. Uncle Herbie went for a smoke to give Winnie and me some privacy to talk. I was scared because everybody was whispering and when they said the word, termination, the words were mouthed but not said out loud. The horror of what I was doing was crushing me and I couldn't stop sobbing. Aunt Winnie told me we would have to go abroad to have the termination performed, no hospital in Ireland would be able to help me, as abortions were illegal. How was I going to explain a random trip away with my aunt to my mum? Winnie had the answer, "Just tell everyone that I'm taking you to see your cousin in England." So, that's what we did and it seemed everyone accepted our story.

I used my savings because I didn't want my aunt Winnie to be out of pocket, after all, she was helping me. I made the journey in a daze, depressed, crying quietly and trying not to draw attention to myself. It was hard to have any meaningful conversation. Winnie understood and when I needed to just sit quietly, she let me. I felt completely alone even though Winnie was right next to me. Every now and then, she leaned over and squeezed my hand tightly. I could tell she was holding back her own tears, trying to be strong for me. We checked into a bed and breakfast. It was small and dingy and I didn't sleep well, how could I? In the morning, we sat in silence at a small breakfast table. I couldn't have anything to eat before the operation. Food was the last thing on my mind and Winnie had lost her appetite too, she had a coffee. There were other people scattered around the small dining area, mostly men who looked like builders. Everyone, getting on with their life. I watched their blurred silhouettes through teary eyes. They weren't taking any notice of us, not aware, what the girl with the red eyes was to endure in a short time. Winnie ordered a taxi to take us to the surgery where the termination was to be performed.

There were several other girls in the waiting room, all looking as scared as I felt. None of us made eye contact, I guessed they were all thinking and feeling the same as me. We all knew we were there for one purpose. We sat silently, staring into space. I felt sad, lonely and guilty. The bad butterflies were grieving with me. A cheerful nurse appeared and walked towards us. "Don't worry darling, it'll be over in a jiffy and you'll be fine." She was very gentle and reassuring. I woke up with a searing pain in my stomach and I was bleeding. Nurse provided me with some strong pain killers telling me this was to be expected and that if I had any concerns I should speak with my own doctor at home. On returning to Ireland my mood didn't change and I remained dazed and depressed. My aunt Winnie tried to comfort me when I repeated how ashamed I felt. "You're not the first girl to have an abortion love and you'll not be the last."

My aunt told me that during and after the first world war, many young girls and women, married or not, would have had either self-induced or back street abortions, some multiple times. She included women labelled as 'barren' or those referred to as a 'spinster' and that they had likely not all been without children. Backstreet abortions sometimes went wrong and some women would have been badly damaged, unable to have children after that. That they would keep that secret and carry it to their grave shocked and saddened me. I began to empathise with other girls I knew, who'd had abortions, those who had given their children up for adoption and those who had given birth and were then forced to pretend a close relative was the parent. I wondered how we would all get our lives back together.

Chapter Nine
The Lady in Red

When I walked into the dance hall, I saw the most beautiful black face I'd ever seen. It was the face of Daniel Daley or Dane as he was nicknamed by his 'squaddie' mates. Dane was a soldier from Yorkshire who had been posted to Northern Ireland. Dane had soft black curly hair cut stylishly and short. He had twinkling eyes and he was looking my way. He approached me for a dance, we got talking and didn't part until the night ended. Dane and I quickly developed a relationship. We gazed lovingly into each other's eyes and he wined and dined me. He was very protective, attentive and caring and acted as if he really loved me. That was a strange feeling because I wasn't used to being loved. "I can't handle this," I told my friend Fran. "Handle what?" she asked loudly. "He's gorgeous and he loves you, what's to handle Annie?" Fran probably thought I was being a drama queen or too picky. I couldn't explain that I didn't feel worth loving. Dane didn't know what I'd done. Although Fran and I were very close, I couldn't even bring myself to confide in her. Because of my secret, I didn't think of myself as a genuine person. When I was complimented, deep down I always thought, if only you knew. The guilt and shame were with me constantly. The secret for me, was like the elephant in the room and it was beginning to affect my behaviour.

My brother Gabriel and I were roughly play fighting in

the sitting room. He pushed me across the room then ran upstairs to hide so that I wouldn't be able to get him back. As I chased after my brother, I heard Timmy come racing upstairs behind me. I could tell by his manic breathing that he was excited and the butterflies warned me I was going to be in trouble. Gabriel had sought sanctuary in the bathroom. I banged furiously on the door, "Gibb, please, please let me in Timmy's gonna bite me." Gibb's eyes appeared from behind a tiny crack in the door. "No!" he said firmly, "I know you're just tryin to get me back." He quickly slammed the door closed in my face.

My body froze readying me for trauma. Timmy leapt up and sank his teeth into my leg. I tried to move and I could feel him imbed them deeper. He was partially wrapped around my lower body, the way I'd seen lions do, when they were killing prey in the Serengeti. When he didn't let go, I dragged him, still hanging on to my leg, to my brother's bedroom, the pain was excruciating. I slowly sat down on the bed, too frightened to cry out. I sat very still until Timmy slowly withdrew his bloodied fangs. He circled in front of me, then sat down and began growling and showing his teeth. I didn't dare to move because even when he sensed me taking in air, he came closer and growled louder, warning me. The blood oozed from the wound and he started licking it. I momentarily thought of Amigo and the sheep. This dog had stalked and tortured me for years and today, I thought he would kill me. I wanted to cover my throat with my hands but I was afraid this would make him attack.

Suddenly, mum burst into the room. She had just returned from shopping. When she saw my leg, she became

193

hysterical and lunged at the dog. I watched in amazement and horror as mum punched him straight in his mouth with such force he yelped out loud. Timmy tried to bite, but she used both hands to choke him, lifting his body up into the air as she did. She had him by the scruff of the neck and began twisting the skin with great force. Timmy's eyes began to bulge and his movements were restricted. He wildly wriggled his lower body, but my mother held tight and thundered downstairs. I don't know how she managed, but she opened the door leading to the passage where the coal shed was, and threw the dog in there. She then slammed the door shut so he couldn't escape.

When Elvid came that day, my mother told him the dog had to go. Elvid chased Timmy with a curtain rail. The dog ran upstairs and crawled under the bed Elvid shared with my mother. Elvid went after him, knelt and using the rod as an extension of his hand he beat Timmy mercilessly. I felt sick at the sight of him savaging that dog. "Please don't beat him anymore," I begged. He stopped when Timmy pissed himself. Elvid dragged him out. The dog's body was shaking uncontrollably, his tail was in a lowered position and his head bowed. He tried not to make eye contact with his master. I had seen the same look of fear many times on the face of my mother. Shortly after, I received stitches to my wounds and Elvid indicated he was moving with Timmy back to his own flat. My life long aim to rid my world of Elvid and his dog had been achieved. He remained my mother's companion, but he never came to my home again. Elvid began to go blind, and ended up in a nursing home before his eventual death there, many years later.

Dane was such a gentleman and apart from deep

meaningful kisses and tender loving caresses, he never pushed things with me. He told me one night, "Annie, I think you are beautiful. The kind of woman a man wants at his side forever. I would never push you into a sexual situation until we are both ready." I couldn't believe my ears. I had wanted to hear these words from a good man all my life. Now that the words were being spoken I was not able to accept them because of my secret. Dane saw the look on my face and thought I'd misunderstood what he meant. He took me by my hands and said, "I mean you are beautiful and I absolutely desire you. You make me feel good, you make me feel warm and you make me feel like a man. But I would never rush things with you because I don't want to lose you. Do you understand?" I didn't answer, but snuggled into him and kissed him passionately.

Dane was taking me out tonight and I wanted to look my best. I squeezed into my long red shoulderless dress. I'd bought it for this special occasion. I thought it showed off my figure and made me look classy. He'd never been to my house before and I was nervous. I didn't want Dane to find out about my mother's drinking. I harassed her all day and she promised to stay sober, joking that I was acting like the queen was coming. When I came out of my room after carefully applying my make-up, mum met me at the bottom of the stairs. "You look beautiful," she slurred, clearly drunk as a skunk. The smile went from my face and the words meant nothing. I was livid that she had dared to get drunk when she knew that Dane was coming and he would meet her for the first time. She'd gone on about how proud she was that I'd met a lovely black man who was in the army. I had no idea she was swigging from a hidden bottle. Where were my butterflies? I remembered my oldest brother's wedding and blamed myself for trusting her. I let her know I was not happy and a shouting match ensued. My mother's mood turned vicious. "Who do you think you are," she screamed. "You are nothing but a black whore, look at the state of you in that dress," she spat. Suddenly I heard a car horn that made me jump. I peeped through the blinds.

Dane opened the door of the cab and made like he was about to get out. I panicked, I didn't want him to see her like this, or hear how she was speaking. I quickly put on my long white fur coat. I ran out and motioned to Dane to get back in the cab, which to my relief he did. As I was running down the path, mum opened the front window and began hurling abuse at me. "You black whore, dirty nigger bitch, what man would want you." I was so ashamed and hurt and mortified that Dane might have heard what she'd said. He stepped out briefly to help me inside the cab, like the gentleman he was telling me how beautiful I looked. "The lady in red," he said dreamily, quoting the title of a song.

"Is that your mum?" he asked, "what was she shouting about?" I didn't answer him. I couldn't speak for fear of bursting into tears. My throat ached with wanting to cry. Dane sensed my discomfort and squeezed my hand. We were ushered to our table in my favourite Chinese restaurant. It was all very awkward and Dane broke the silence. "What is it Annie, have I done something, you've been quiet all night." I couldn't bear it any longer, my mother's words were suffocating me, I couldn't believe what she'd said. I burst into floods of tears and Dane was stunned. He held me tightly and gently asked again what the matter was. I couldn't tell him the truth, so I said that mum and I had argued and that I was feeling upset. I didn't dare tell him what she'd said how could I? How could this gentle and normal human being understand my life with her? I excused myself and ran into the ladies where I cried uncontrollably, I just couldn't stop. I returned to my lovely companion with red puffy eyes and shaking hands. My make-up had faded and I felt ugly and tired. That night Dane told me how much he adored me and cared for me.

"Well?" enquired Fran with excitement, "did he give it to you last night?" "Did who give me what?" I asked puzzled. "Dane, Dane, did he give you the ring Annie, come on don't keep me in suspense." "What ring, what are you talking about?" I was astonished as Fran told how Dane had bought me an engagement ring saying that he wanted to marry me. He had sworn Fran to secrecy not to say a word to me. When I phoned Dane, he said that he had the ring in his pocket and had wanted to ask for my hand in marriage. When he saw how emotional I was after my arguing with my mum, he decided that the time was not right. "You looked so beautiful but so sad," he said. "I'll never forget that dress," he repeated the quote, "the lady in red." Although I wasn't ready to marry Dane, I was very flattered he loved me enough to ask. I was confused and didn't know how to move forward with Dane. I began to push him away. Dane and I slowly drifted apart and he eventually went back to Yorkshire. We kept in touch by letter, for a while. I didn't know how to handle Dane's love and he didn't know how to handle my rejection. Although I didn't know it then, we were to be reacquainted more than two decades later.

My grandfather was ill and he had his first stroke. This left him partially paralysed down one side. He dribbled when he tried to talk and his hand was limp. It was hard watching him like that. "Get me some bleach love," he called after I had washed his face and hands and given him a change of clothes. "What for granddad?" "Be a good girl now, and just get the bleach for me. Put it in an egg cup and bring me a matchstick." He told me to busy myself and not to come in the room until he called for me. I was bewildered, but did as he asked. He shouted that it was ok for me to come back in the room again. "Well love, anything different about your old grandda?" His smiled as wide as he could. "Oh, God granddad, please tell me you didn't." But he had. He had put bleach on a matchstick and cleaned his teeth with it. "Don't I look just as handsome as I did years ago?" I laughed, "Yes granddad you do." I worried about my grandfather a lot. He was the most important person in my life. He had been my saviour, my friend and my adopted father throughout my childhood. I would rush to his home from work to ensure that he was fed and that his house was clean and tidy.

A few months later, granddad had another stroke. He became so weak, that my uncles and brother had to turn the dining room into a bed-sit for him. He had to be carried upstairs to have a bath by my brothers and my uncles. Billy Gracey didn't like this one bit. I'd just put some meat in the oven and I was coming out of the kitchen. I listened, thinking I'd heard an unusual sliding noise. I looked to where the noise was coming from, and realised it was from the stairs. I thought, we might be being burgled. Slowly I made my way to the hall. I held my breath and peeked through the crack in the door. To my horror, there was my grandfather trying to pull himself upstairs.

"What the heck are you doing grandda?" I screamed.

"I want to have a bath by myself," he cried. "I've got my pride left you know."

"But you're not very well and you might hurt yourself."

"Outta my way chile."

"Alan," I shouted.

"What's the matter?"

"Come quickly its grandda."

My grandfather was not pleased I had raised the alarm. I was afraid for him, and decided to move in with him. This was a chance to get away from my needy family. I initially enjoyed being away from them, but I began to miss home. I thought about my life with my mother and brothers. I missed the hustle and bustle of daily life and I missed the noise. Whatever we had gone through, we had always been together. I didn't know any other way of life, and despite being sick of them sometimes, I still loved them. I loved them all, mum, Gabriel, Wilson and Wee Bill. My mum shocked the hell out of me and she said she would stop drinking, if I'd come home. She cried with happiness when I finally relented and returned after work one day. Although I hadn't been away for long, things seemed different and the house felt unfamiliar. My life seemed disorganised and without routine. The butterflies told me that change was afoot. I got the feeling that things would never be the same again.

I was called to the office in work. "Your cousin Ida has just phoned," said Mr Lal, one of the factory's executive directors. He looked sympathetically at me and before he uttered another word I instinctively knew he'd gone. I was driven home in silence. On the way, I reminisced. I remembered him wearing his trilby hat, cocked on one side like a gangster. I remembered how I used to go with my granddad to the big open fields next to Hoy's Meadow. We spent so many lovely moments there with his dogs. I remembered the haircut he'd given me with the dog shears. I remembered my grandfather's kindness, his grumpy voice when he was angry, his mischievous twinkling eyes and his lop-sided grin. I heard Mr Lal's gentle voice. "We're here dear. Do you want me to come inside?" I shook my head and thanked him for his kindness.

I felt cold as I entered his room. The last time we spoke, he asked me to peel a pear for him and he wanted a drink of 'Adam's Ale'. He jokingly said this referring to water. He said he had asked the Lord for forgiveness and he wanted his bible. He had a calmness about him and said he was ready to be with his wife. "Come and see him love, he's still warm," said my mum. I touched his face gently, and indeed he still was warm. A few nights before, I had held that soft wrinkled hand of his. He had whispered his love for me, and told me not to cry. I tried very hard, but I broke down and sobbed like a baby. I sensed he was nearing the end of his life and he was trying to say goodbye to me. I didn't want to hear, I didn't want to believe that I might soon walk into this room never to see or hear him again. No, no, no! I had severe pain in my heart and my head pounded. Now, looking at him, I felt lost and alone. "Don't leave me granddad," I whispered.

I didn't attend his funeral because I couldn't bear to watch his body being lowered into the ground, it was too final. I thought, if I didn't see that, I could somehow pretend he was still alive. I needed to hear his voice again. I wanted to see the sparkle in his eyes again as he laughingly recalled stories of his childhood days to me. I wanted to touch his hands, I wanted to hug him. I wanted to replay his last hours so there might be a different outcome and he was still here. Or at least hear him say he loved me, one last time ... Gabriel and I had talked to him, when he was lying in his coffin. I can't recall what we said. Now I couldn't remember if I'd told him that I loved him, before he passed and I was annoyed with myself. I hope he knew I loved him. Part of my life was gone, forever. I couldn't talk about my granddad without crying and I left the room if others mentioned his name. At the time, I didn't understand this was grief. Alan and my two uncles still lived in his house, but I didn't want to be in there without my granddad, and I rarely visited.

Heads bowed ... Rock of ages, cleft for me ... I didn't want to hear the rest; my rock had gone. Goodbye granddad ... until we meet again ...

Because of all the mythical tales I'd been told as a child, I grew up with a fear of death and ghosts. When there was a death, some would take great pleasure in telling listening children, that their ghost would come back to haunt us. My grandfather's death was playing on my mind and I was afraid. When I came home from work, if no-one else had gotten there before me, I would sit outside on the cold concrete step, too afraid to go inside in case a ghost came to me. I jumped at unexpected noises and didn't sleep well. I had nightmares and I was generally unhappy. One night when I had been brave enough to go inside alone I stopped what I'd been doing to listen to the rain. Ever since I was a little girl the sound of rain held a certain comfort for me. In Florence Court, I listened to the rain's pitter patter, as it descended onto the tin roof of our coal shed. When we had moved to Killicomaine, the coal shed was inside the property and was therefore out of the rain. I'd tried to recreate this gentle and soothing sound by placing an empty can on my bedroom window ledge.

My attempts failed, as the wind usually blew the can off the ledge and into the darkness of the garden below. Tonight, the rain sounded menacing and when I heard the first clap of thunder I hid behind the blinds and started crying for my mother. She was distressed when she returned, finding me curled up inside one of the curtains shaking. "It's gonna get me ma, it's gonna get me," I sobbed. My mum put her arms around me and looking puzzled she said, "It's alright love it's only thunder. Nothing's gonna get you." My family started to notice my odd behaviour and mum was concerned. She spoke to my aunt Winnie about me being frightened all the time.

Aunt Winnie sat me down on the sofa and held me gently by my hands. "Look at me Annie." I did as she asked. "What's the matter love, what is it?" I burst into tears as I explained that I couldn't get my grandfather out of my mind. I said that ever since I had seen his dead body I walked around in constant fear. "What is there to be afraid of love?" I couldn't answer because I didn't know. All I did know was that everywhere I went I was gripped with a fear that caused me to have an ache in my belly constantly and something that felt like tingling nerves in my chest. Many years later, I learned these were panic attacks. "Did your grandda ever do you any harm when he was alive?" asked Winnie. "No, never," I replied. "Well then, he'll never do you any harm now that he's dead, will he?"

I felt reassured after my aunt Winnie finished speaking with me. I still had the odd flutter of nerves in my stomach on hearing unexpected noises but I could be at home alone and I began to sleep a little better. Things still weren't right though and I had endless dreams about my grandfather. I had a recurring dream that he came to me in my garden, where everything was white and peaceful. Granddad had grown a white beard and resembled Santa Clause. There was no noise just granddad and me sitting together on a sleigh being pulled by a reindeer riding round and round the garden together. My granddad was smiling and never took his eyes off my face. Everything in the dream played in slow motion and in the dream I was happy again. I cried when I woke up because I wanted to be with my grandfather.

Chapter Ten

Death and Life

Thoughts of my granddad were a constant on my mind. Everywhere I turned, there seemed to be laughter, but I wasn't laughing, I felt sad, lonely and depressed. I couldn't tell anyone because I was afraid they wouldn't care and that would be too much to bear. I didn't think they would understand. I went to work, came home at six, ate, washed and slept. At weekends, I forced myself to go to all the usual haunts with my friends and I pretended to enjoy myself. I was a good actress and I hid my pain very well, I thought I had to. Annie Yellowe was the life and soul of the party. Annie made people laugh, but I was crying inside and feeling desperate. Every day, I was inexplicably anxious and the butterflies mercilessly ate my stomach. Over the years, I had developed an understanding of the butterflies, I knew they were trying to warn me, but I didn't understand their message, maybe I didn't want to. I was drinking more at weekends to mask my real feelings and quieten the butterflies, I longed for respite from their vicious presence. It all unexpectedly came to a head one night, whilst I was with friends in the factory's bar.

As was usual, the bar was full and noisy. There were half empty glasses of Guinness and spirits on every table. Cigarette smoke was thick in the air. People were singing, laughing and joking. We sat near the door. One of my male friends, jokingly asked when he and I would finally make mad passionate love. He teased me a lot, and usually I took this in good spirits, giving as good as I got. But the butterflies told me I should feel insulted by his comments. They gripped my stomach with such force, I suddenly choked up. I fought hard to control myself, but I felt fragile, so very fragile. I couldn't speak and finally, the lump in my throat gave way and I burst into tears. He tried to comfort me, begging me to believe he was only joking and would never say anything to hurt me. I ran from the bar and made my way towards home. My head was spinning and all the sad, bad pieces of my life flashed through my mind.

The night was dark, cold and wet. As I walked, I passed the Pleasure Gardens. I heard the laughter and saw the children playing on the swings and making daisy chains. I thought of the bodies in the river Bann and Hoy's Meadow. I passed the antique shop where I'd tried to sell my doll. Just to the right was the launderette where I'd learned to question my family ties. I looked across the road to where my neighbours had gathered to beat Catholics on their way to and from work. I passed the bar where my mother drank, where I'd entertained my friends, impersonating people and where James Liggett lost his life. Further on, I touched the walls of my old primary, the gloomy building now vacant and where I'd been humiliated as a child. I reached the Batchelor's Walk where I'd played and climbed trees and where Sam Johnston lost his life. I passed the fields where we played spin the bottle and kiss chase. I thought of Andrew. I heard blowing horns in the distance as cars swerved to avoid me. I continued to cross roads recklessly not caring whether I was run over. Nearing my front door, I thought about my Amigo. I saw his little face as a puppy. I remembered him looking back as he walked to his death. I thought about my failed relationship with Dane, my aborted child and my grandfather's passing. I needed the pain to go away, I wanted the world to STOP and let me off!

I went upstairs to my bedroom and changed into my night-dress and dressing gown. I picked up a towel and went downstairs to the kitchen. I turned on the gas cooker without lighting it. I placed the folded towel inside the oven and lay down inhaling the fumes deeply. Our father who art in heaven ...I began to feel very relaxed and sleepy. Through the haze, I had fleeting thoughts of regret and that I didn't want to die. I wanted to get up, but the fumes kept me still. Suddenly, the back door burst open and I saw blurred figures in front of me. All around me was in slow motion. Mouths moved, but words came much later. I felt my body being lifted and heard someone shout, "Annie, Annie. Oh, my God, put your fag out before you blow us all up ... open the windows, call an ambulance."

I came around on a cold white trolley, surrounded by doctors and nurses. My body hurt, my mouth was dry and I was shaking. I mumbled that I was fine and wanted to go home. Doctor told me, "I think you should stay overnight and see a psychiatrist in the morning." "Me, see a shrink, you must be joking, I'm not mad. No thank you, I want to go home." Doctor was not pleased that I had 'wasted his time'. Alan had gotten married and they'd had their first son, Dillan. He had moved out of my granddad's old home and moved into a new modern property. I slept on Alan's sofa that night. In the morning, he brought me breakfast, two boiled eggs and buttered toast. "What's wrong love, are you pregnant?" "Pregnant," I laughed bitterly, and shook my head. I had flashes of the abortion. "No, I'm not pregnant, I answered wearily. I'm stuck and unhappy with my life. I'm sad, so sad and so tired of everything." My brother tried to comfort me and said life was not that bad and we had to make the most of it. I knew he wouldn't understand my life and I didn't blame him. My life was so different from the life he and my older brother Jimmy had. I needed to get out of Ireland, away from the troubles, the ignorance and the sadness. I felt ashamed of what I had tried to do, I didn't mean it. I realised it was a cry for help because I didn't think anyone was noticing my grief. I became focussed about leaving Ireland for good. For a time, everyone tip-toed around me, trying not to upset me, just in case … I tried to assure them that I would never try the same thing again, that I had it all under control now. I would be strong again and sort out my life with dignity.

It was Andrew who helped me to begin to put my life in perspective and concentrate on my own needs. He knew that I had tried to take my life. Andrew knocked on my bedroom door. I told him to go away and pushed my tear stained face into my pillow. He eased the door open, and came right in. He perched himself on the edge of my bed then, gently lifted my head and cradled me. Andrew said he was hurting for me and could see how much I'd changed. "Jesus Christ Annie, you are a beautiful person, you need to start looking after yourself more." "But they all need me, they can't cope without me." No!" said Andrew firmly. He told me to start looking after … Numero Uno, number one, and that my family would learn to cope without my support. I was about to make a decision that would change my life beyond recognition and for ever.

Wilson had moved to London and we spoke on the phone most Sunday's. "Come over for a break," he pleaded. Wilson was aware of my somewhat, fragile state. He lived in a squat with several friends. I was surprised to know that squatting was practised in England, and was not illegal at that time. I was meticulous about cleanliness and I didn't think I could live in a squat. Queen Bee, that's what my brothers called me, because I was so house-proud. My brother laughed and assured me his squat was clean and had all the necessary amenities. He reeled off a list, as if he was making a sale. "I'll make sure you stay in the best room," he said. I was reassured and said I'd come.

In work, I'd been speaking to my friend Kate, about my plans. She was excited and encouraged me. Kate said she too was longing for change and asked if she could come with me. I thought this was a great idea, because like me, Kate was hard working, fun and feisty. She was younger than me and I said she should check with her mother first. We hardly did any work that day and constantly sneaked into each other's isle to fantasise about London. We decided to do a trial weekend, with a view to moving there permanently, if things worked out. We went together to Kate's home and she was given her mother's permission with the understanding, I would look after her.

Wilson met Kate and I, at Heathrow. As soon as we came into view he shouted, "Soda!" Soda was my childhood nickname. Wilson and Gabriel called me Soda, especially when they were being protective or affectionate and they still use it to this day. He threw his arms around my neck and hugged me tightly, smiling and kissing me over and over. We were like two little pups being reacquainted. Wilson and I were very alike and missed each other's company and fun. He knew Kate well and finally turned to greet and kiss her too, sweeping her up off her feet and into the air, as he did so. Wilson was full of beans as always and couldn't wait to show us around London.

When the doors of the tube opened, I stood back as it was packed with commuters. Wilson shouted, "come on Soda," and dragged us inside. We squeezed ourselves into a corner, or rather, Wilson shuffled us in there. I think we were the noisiest people on the tube. Heads slowly turned to look in our direction as we cackled and chatted loudly, in our strong Irish accent. After a long journey, we reached the Elephant and Castle. As we stepped out of the tube station, Wilson pointed upwards and shouted, "look sis, that's the pink elephant I was telling you about." He walked us a short distance to a block of flats, around twenty stories high. I was worried there wouldn't be a lift. Wilson slapped me playfully on the back, "Look at your face. Don't worry Soda we're on the first floor." Like an estate agent, he showed us every room and assured us there would be constant lighting and hot water. "We've rigged up free electricity," he roared with laughter. I hoped we wouldn't all get electrocuted but my brother was rushing us to freshen up. He had things to show us.

I will never forget the feelings inside me, when Wilson took me to the West End for the first time. My butterflies went crazy, dancing with joy and I didn't want to calm them. My senses were on alert and I was in awe at the new sights before me, the buildings, the shops, the smells, the noise and the ethnic mix of people. I walked next to people who didn't stare at me. Every time I saw a black woman or man, I looked at them with pride and smiled widely, I said hello cheerily to all. My brother tried to help me to contain myself, but he failed. Some said hello back, some side stepped me with caution and some of the guys followed me for a few yards. On Regent Street, I looked to my right and spotted a huge luxurious coach passing by. Inside there were more than a dozen black men dressed in cool navy suits with colour coordinated light blue shirts. I thought they might be football or cricket players. I sighed the deepest sigh of relief at this sight. I'd never seen so many other black people in one place before. In Ireland, my brothers and I were ALWAYS the only black people on the buses. For the first time in my life, I was experiencing what I'd dreamed of as normal.

I had a flash of myself looking in the mirror as a child, trying to speak with an English accent, pinching my nose, thinking the look made me more acceptable, trying to scrub myself white, for the same reason and in failing to fit, wanting to get away to be me . . . Annie Yellowe! I loved this feeling, I wanted this feeling to stay with me for the rest of my life.

Back at work on Monday morning, and I just couldn't settle. "If I pull this bobbin of wool around anymore, I'm going to scream," I thought. I looked across at Kate, she was crying. Walking up and down her little isle, expertly looking for faults in her carpet. Kate wiped the tears from her eyes, looked over at me, then came running over. "Let's go," she said excitedly. "Come on Annie, let's get the fuck out of this piss hole." "Are you sure, I asked? . . . "Let's go."

Before I knew it, I was out of there, back home and packing my bags for London. I was nervous but I was happy. I said farewell to all my friends at work, amidst playful shouts of, "she'll be back in a week, she'll never last, see you next week Annie."

They sent me off with some gifts, perfumed soaps and a red vanity case. My stomach churned as I looked at my reflection in the mirror. "Is that me, that pale and lost looking young woman with the big red eyes?" Mum started sobbing as I walked out the door. I gave her a cuddle and said, "sorry mum, but I have to go. I don't belong here, I never have." Now it was time for her to grow up and stop hanging on to my apron strings. "Be a big girl," I teased. Mum tried to laugh through her tears. Poor mum, a tiny frail looking little woman, standing at the window watching part of her life disappearing down the path, possibly forever. I took long deep breaths, I would not cry, no I would not. After all, I was embarking on a journey towards normality. My mind was racing with doubts but it was too late, the people of Ireland faded into matchstick men and women, the buildings to tiny dots as the aircraft soared up into the air and snuggled in between the fluffy white clouds.

I tried to sum up my life to this point. My home had been transformed by me, with nice things I'd previously craved. I was employed, something I feared I'd never accomplish. I worked four jobs, the one in the Ulster Carpet Mills factory, myself and two friends, who were sisters, cleaned the factory's attached bar, we served behind that bar and we waited on tables in there. Now I was starting all over again.

I thought of 31 Florence Court, where we lived as children and where my journey in Ireland first began. When I was about seven years old, I was combing my mother's long black hair. She was sat on a wooden chair, in front of the fire, in the middle of our sitting room. My mother loved having her hair combed. I was as usual, day dreaming. I turned to my mother and said, "mum, when I grow up I'm gonna write a book about us." My mother laughed gently and touched my hand with hers, as if to say, 'bless her'.

"What makes you think people would be interested in us love?"

"I don't think other black people live the same way we do."

She smiled, stretching her hand out again and patting mine, she said,

"Yes, you tell them love, warts and all."

FOR THE LOVE OF A MOTHER ...

CPSIA information can be obtained
at www.ICGtesting.com
Printed in the USA
FSOW01n0710200417
33347FS

9 781909 465565